INTRODUCTION TO INTERNATIONAL AIR LAW

STUDENT'S GUIDE

COMMON GROUND

First published in 2024
as part of the Interdisciplinary Social Sciences Book Imprint
http://doi.org/10.18848/978-1-963049-34-3/CGP (Full Book)

Common Ground Research Networks
2001 South First St, Suite 201 L
University of Illinois Research Park
Champaign, IL
61820

Library of Congress Cataloging-in-Publication Data

Names: Mbuzukongira, Gracieux, author.
Title: Introduction to International Air Law : Student's Guide / Gracieux
    Mbuzukongira.
Description: Champaign : Common Ground Research Networks, 2024. | Series:
    International Law Teaching Pocketbook Series; vol 1 | Includes
    bibliographical references and index. | Summary: "This student guide is
    designed for students and practitioners in the legal and aviation
    industries. Its simple and clear language makes it easy for readers
    without prior legal knowledge as it remains relevant for experts in the
    legal field. The book discusses various international air navigation
    principles as provided by the 1944 Chicago Convention and its annexes.
    It further discusses the Warsaw system of liability before it discusses
    the International Civil Aviation Organization (ICAO) and the
    International Air Transport Association (IATA)"-- Provided by publisher.

Identifiers: LCCN 2024012992 (print) | LCCN 2024012993 (ebook) | ISBN
    9781963049329 (hardback) | ISBN 9781963049336 (paperback) | ISBN
    9781963049343 (adobe pdf)
Subjects: LCSH: Aeronautics--Law and legislation. | Aeronautics,
    Commercial--Law and legislation.
Classification: LCC K4095 .M39 2024 (print) | LCC K4095 (ebook) | DDC
    343.09/7--dc23/eng/20240325
LC record available at https://lccn.loc.gov/2024012992
LC ebook record available at https://lccn.loc.gov/2024012993

Cover Photo Credit: Phillip Kalantzis Cope

There was neither hammer nor ax nor any tool of iron heard in the house, because a certain worm called shamir split everything noiselessly, and thus, they did not require other tools.

THE ZOHAR

ACKNOWLEDGEMENT

No one can attain any small achievement on their own, without any support. Indeed, wisdom teaches that we only give because we have received in the first place; thus, our sages would say that it is out of what is in Your hands that we are giving you.

My interest in air law can be traced back to the years I spent on campus during my master's studies at the University of Nairobi. It is, thus, obvious that I would first thank my mentor, The Hon. Prof. Dr. Abraham Kithure Kindiki, for having groomed me in this area.

I recall how particular our circumstances were, and how much I then benefited from various people, including one of my classmates, The Hon. Emeritus Deputy Chief Justice Dr. Nancy Baraza, to whom I say *tenda wema nenda zako*. (After you do a good deed, you leave it at that.)

I should express how grateful I am to my elder sister, Odette Polepole Mbuzukongira, who generously accepted to sponsor this research. In addition, she regularly checked on me and would always whisper encouraging words.

As any teacher would say, my students are not aware of how much they have taught me. I regret that I am unable to mention your names here, but kindly accept my appreciation for the opportunity you granted me to learn with you. This goes for the students I taught yesterday, the ones I am currently teaching, and the ones I will teach tomorrow.

In a particular way, I would like to thank Prof. Dr. Mathias Sahinkuye of the African Institute of International Law and Patricia Alonso for the sacrifice they made at the very last of the publication of this book—your advise has been invaluable to me.

Last, but certainly not least, I shall forever remain grateful to G-d for the wonderful family He has given me; nothing encourages me more than seeing daughters and sons around me! May He reward you abundantly!

The success of this project has a name, like all my previous projects did: Lydia woke me up when I had no courage left. She gave me a reason to push forward when I had none. She initiated ideas when I had none. No words can express my gratitude to you.

TABLE OF CONTENTS

INTRODUCTION

International air law might be considered one of the recent developments in international law; it is, however, one of its fastest growing branches. The importance of international air law cannot be overstated as the extent to which human activities rely on air transport for moving either passengers or cargo is evident.

Other than it being an important field, the International Civil Aviation Organization has recently estimated that the demand for air transport will increase by an average of 4.3 percent per annum over the next 20 years.[1] The growth in the aviation industry is explained by many factors, including recent technological discoveries, but also by the global trend in human interaction that has developed social and economic ties, which comes with the need for more mobility. Such developments require prompt and timely regulations to address the various challenges that accompany them.

This book is but a minor contribution to raising awareness in the field of air law through various topics discussed, including its historical development, the various freedoms of air, the rules of environmental protection, the security of aircraft, the air traffic control service, aircraft search and rescue, the Rules of the Air, and the Warsaw System of Liability. Two institutions have proven their relevance concerning air transport—the International Civil Aviation Organization (ICAO) and the International Air Transport Association (IATA)—and they are discussed in this book.

Various sources of law were considered during this research, from norms of international customary law to treaties and conventions duly ratified by States parties but mainly the 1944 Chicago Convention on International Civil Aviation, which, for reasons didactic, is an appendix to this book. Alongside these sources, various annexes to the Convention, together with the Standards and Recommended Practices (SARPs) for international civil aviation as they have been adopted within the framework of ICAO, constitute the main source of this research.

This research has equally relied on other sources of law, including decisions of courts of law and quasi-judicial mechanisms, as it has benefited from various scholarly writings published in leading international and national periodicals, journals, newspapers, reports, aide-mémoire, *travaux préparatoires* (preparatory works), and reference works, as well as other relevant data available.

A twofold method was used for this research: a theoretical approach reflecting on the actual creation of legal rules and an implementation-focused approach reflecting on the observance and application of legal rules and the successes achieved in strengthening legality and the consolidation of the law.

As defined by Banakar and Travers,[2] the rule-based paradigm, which consists of a study of law with recourse to the exegesis authoritative argument that allows one to read and to criticize its content, has been of great use for this research.

CHAPTER 1

Definition and Historical Development

1. Definition

No international treaty has till date defined the concept of air law; however, scholarship has filled in this gap by providing various definitions for the same. Thus, Diederiks-Verschoor suggests that air law is to be understood as "a body of rules governing the use of airspace and its benefits for aviation, the general public, and the nations of the world."[1]

Michael Milde traces the origin of the concept of air law back to the work of the Institut de Droit International in the early 1900s, which might have coined the concept of air law. He suggests that the concept of aeronautical law would have been more precise, considering that air law would include all the usage of air space, including regulations of wireless transmission or propagation of electromagnetic waves through space, the use of wind power to generate electricity, and protection from air pollution.[2]

Cheng defines the concept of air law to mean part of international air law that relates to civil aviation, including international institutions concerned with air law. Thus, the concept of aviation shall be understood to include all aspects related to the operation and use of aircraft; however, this concept excludes hovercraft, as it does not include air pollution; telecommunication and military aviation; and sometimes State's aircrafts.[3] As defined by the *Max-Planck Encyclopedia of International Public Law*, States' aircrafts are understood as aircrafts owned and operated by the government.[4]

This broad definition finds its basis in two dimensions: the ownership and the utilization of the aircraft. However, in practice, if an aircraft is used for civil purposes, it should be considered a civil aircraft, and if it is used for State purposes, it is considered a State aircraft. An aircraft is used for State purposes if it is controlled by the State and exclusively performs a public task or service.

2. Historical Development

The history of legislation of air law can be traced back to April 23, 1784 in France, when the Lieutenant de la Police de Paris issued a directive according to which, in heavily populated areas, no balloons were to be flown without prior police authorization. Such legislation followed the experience of the Montgolfier Brothers, who had successfully flown unguided air balloons.[5] However, the uncertainty which was caused by the lack of experience in this newly discovered area would prompt the police directive.

Indeed, a series of experiences of flying balloons had taken place in France as two brothers, Joseph-Michel and Etienne Jacques Montgolfier, were trying to demonstrate their invention. For example, they launched a balloon on June 4, 1783 in Annonay with nobody on board,[6] and another one on September 19, 1783 in Versailles with only a sheep, a rooster, and a duck on board.[7] The brothers would launch the first crewed flight a month later, with a balloon with one person on board, Jean-François Pilâtre de Rozier, a chemistry and physics teacher.[8] It would take another month to have two persons—Jean-François Pilâtre de Rozier and the Marquis d'Arlandes, a French military officer—on board a hot air balloon, flying from the center of Paris to the suburbs on November 21, 1783.[9]

As these experiences became more frequent, 1852 emerged as a breakthrough year in the aviation industry with Henry Giffard installing a steam engine on a balloon to move its propeller with a directed arm, creating the first dirigible airship and moving passengers over France.

It is important to note that the aforementioned police directive was a piece of legislation applicable at the domestic level; internationally, the first attempt at the codification of international air law could be traced to the time when German balloons made flights above French territory. Following such an attempt in the early 1900s, the French government proposed that the two governments secure an agreement on the matter. This proposal led to the Paris Agreement of 1910.[10]

It should be indicated that there had been other discussions on the matter. Indeed, the Final Act of the Hague Peace Conference of 1899 had already prohibited the discharge of projectiles and explosives from balloons. However, such efforts are rather considered part of the historical development of air warfare and are not part of the historical development of civil aviation law.[11]

2.1 The 1910 Paris Conference

Although the International Air Navigation Conference held in Paris from May 10 to June 29, 1910 has never been celebrated as a success, it has nevertheless been recorded as the first diplomatic conference on civil aviation, and its outcome has heavily influenced subsequent legislation in air law. For instance, the principle that airspace above the territory of a State is part of the sovereignty of that State is now accepted as part of international customary law. This principle had already been agreed upon during the 1910 Paris Conference.[12]

The background of the 1910 Paris Conference was the lack of any form of control over balloons, which, at that time, were taking off and landing freely across Europe in an unregulated manner and which, at some point, caused concerns to the French after more than a dozen German balloons had crossed into France, some of them flown by German military officers in November 1908.

The work of the 1910 Paris Conference would result in the first bilateral agreement on international air services, signed between France and Germany in 1913.[13] However, the European political context of the time did not allow the Paris Conference to be crowned by success as it otherwise could have been. The work of the Conference would have to wait until the end of WWI to be revised and adopted further by the 1919 Convention.

2.2 The 1919 Convention Relating to the Regulation of Aerial Navigation

The 1919 Convention will have the merit of having codified some of the international norms that constitute the backbone of civil aviation today. For instance, in its Article 1, the Convention states, "The High contracting Parties recognize that every Power has complete and exclusive sovereignty over the air space above its territory." Its Article 2 further states, "Each contracting State undertakes in time of peace to accord freedom of innocent passage above its territory to the aircraft of the other contracting States, provided that the conditions laid down in the present Convention are observed."

Thus, early commentators on the 1919 Convention then high-lighted the fact that "in the international sphere this theory of complete national sovereignty in the air space has triumphed, and that the growing practice is to create by convention a mutual right of passage for non-military aircraft, and it can be only a short time before that practice becomes universal as between all states which have recognized one another and one another's govern-ments."[14] Sure enough, this prediction came to pass, as will be discussed here.

Furthermore, the 1919 Convention would have a double merit: first, for having laid down the idea of the necessity of the in-ternational uniformity of air law, and second, for the creation of the International Commission for Air Navigation as a permanent body not only to monitor the implementation of the Convention but also to permanently study possible improvements to the Con-vention.[15]

Indeed, the need for the establishment of a uniform legal regime in air law cannot be overstated, as explained by Albert Roper, the then general secretary of the Commission:

> No international air traffic would be possible if a pilot flying, say, from London to India, had to comply with six or twelve dif-ferent systems of regulations, and the safety of the flights would be seriously reduced if the airmen had to obey various rules of countries whose boundaries they could not even see from the air, and had to use different maps and understand different codes of meteorological information.[16]

It is important to note that the uniformity of norms of air law is not only a matter of international law, as such uniformity is reflected even in national legislation. Thus, for instance, Article 13 of the 1919 Convention recognizes the competence of States to issue certificates of airworthiness and of competency, and licenses. However, it requires that such documents be issued as per regulations established by the relevant annexes.

Nevertheless, it should be indicated that the 1919 Convention did not escape the political influence of the moment, which would have some implications on the position of Germany toward the Convention. For instance, the Inter-Allied Aeronautical Commission created by the Paris Peace Conference of 1919 had been mandated to prepare a convention on international aerial navigation in time of peace.[17] As Dempsey explains, the Treaty of Versailles had already given the Allied Forces a full liberty of passage and landing over and in Germany, which ipso facto required the recognition of their certificate of nationality and airworthiness.[18]

Thus, Article 5 of the 1919 Convention provided the following:

> No contracting State shall, except by a special and temporary authorization, permit the flight above its territory of an aircraft which does not possess the nationality of a contracting State unless it has concluded a special convention with the State in which the aircraft is registered.[19]

However, such an article was quickly amended to read, "Each contracting State is entitled to conclude special conventions with non-contracting States. The stipulations of such special conventions shall not infringe the rights of the contracting parties to the present Convention."

Another political element would be reflected in the position of Spain, which did not adhere to the 1919 Convention, as Spain considered herself not satisfied with the political position she held vis-à-vis other European States. Because of such dissatisfaction, Spain initiated her diplomatic negotiations on civil aviation, which culminated in the 1926 Ibero-American Convention of Aerial Navigation. This Convention was signed in Madrid and reflected nearly a copy of the 1919 Convention, except that it only emanated from Spain and included some Latin America States. However, the 1926 Madrid Convention never entered into force and was abandoned.

2.3 The 1928 Havana Convention on Commercial Aviation

Initiated by the United States, the Pan-American Commission for Aerial Navigation first met in 1927 to prepare the Pan-American Convention on Aerial Navigation. The Commission worked on its assignment tirelessly, resulting in the Convention that was signed in Havana on February 20, 1928 and that entered into force on June 13, 1929. It is interesting to note that most of the States parties had also signed the 1926 Madrid Convention.

Nevertheless, certain aspects of the 1928 Havana Convention are worth special attention. For instance, Article 1, recognizes that every State has complete and exclusive sovereignty over the airspace above its territory and territorial waters. Article 4 grants freedom of innocent passage above its territory to private aircrafts of the other contracting State, although under the conditions provided by the Convention.

It could be said that the novel aspect of the 1928 Havana Convention was that learning from previous efforts, the Convention progressively opened up the skies of its States parties; for instance, in its Article 18 (3), it stipulated that "[e]ach and every contracting state shall notify every other party to this convention and the Pan-American Union of such airports as shall be designated by such State as ports of entry and departure." It introduces the question of liabilities in Article 28, saying that reparations and damages caused to persons or property located in the subjacent territory shall be governed by the laws of each State party.

Whereas Article 31 calls for possible cooperation on relevant issues, including meteorological information, aeronautical charts, and radiotelegraph in aerial navigation, Article 32 calls for uniformity of laws and regulations governing aerial navigation within States parties. Thus, as stated by Stephen Latchford, the 1928 Havana Convention was designed to meet conditions existing in Europe and to permit gradual adoption of such rules and regulations in conformity with the principles established by the Convention.[20]

However, the Convention suffers from a shortcoming of not establishing an implementation and monitoring institution.

CHAPTER 2

The 1944 Chicago Convention and the Freedoms of Air

Considered the backbone of international air law, the 1944 Chicago Convention could be divided into two parts: the international legal framework of civil aviation and the constitution of the ICAO.

The 1944 Chicago Convention is indeed hailed as the "landmark agreement establishing the core principles permitting international transport by air."[1] However, the merit of the Convention has been that it rather capitalized on the existing principles that were already universally accepted. In addition, the Convention equally developed new rules of air navigation, including some freedoms of air navigation.

2.1 The First Freedom: The Freedom to Fly

The first freedom of air is understood as the right granted by one State to another State to fly across its territory without landing. Practice might suggest that States have been jealously keeping their eyes up, watching over their skies so that no unauthorized aircraft may fly over a State without prior permission.

Article 5 of the 1944 Chicago Convention provides the following:

> Each contracting State agrees that all aircraft of the other contracting States, being aircraft not engaged in scheduled international air services, shall have the right, subject to the observance of the terms of this Convention, to make flights into or in transit non-stop across its territory and to make stops for non-traffic purposes without the necessity of obtaining prior permission, and subject to the right of the State flown over to require landing.

Indeed, for the nonscheduled flight, the freedom to fly, albeit having been provided by the aforementioned article, is subjected by the same article to the right of the State being overflown. This might be construed as a tacit requirement indicating that no State can be flown over without such State having granted prior permission, as will be discussed later.

2.2 The Second Freedom: Non-traffic Landing Freedom

The second freedom applies when a State grants to another State the freedom to land in its territory for non-traffic purposes during its scheduled international flights. A non-traffic stop is understood as a technical stop. At the time when aircrafts were unable to fly for a long range without refueling or taking care of other services and maintenance-related issues, States would agree on such non-traffic stops. During a non-traffic stop, the airline is not allowed to embark or disembark passengers, cargo, or mails.

The concept of non-traffic stop might have been overtaken by the latest inventions in the aircraft industry, whereby the newly invented Mach 5 hypersonic engine is five times faster than the speed of the sound and, thus, capable of crossing the ocean in half a day without needing any refueling or maintenance.

2.3 The Third Freedom: Freedom to Discharge

While the first two freedoms are non-traffic freedoms, the freedom to discharge is a traffic freedom. This freedom allows a scheduled international flight to discharge its passengers, cargo, and mails.

When a scheduled international flight is engaged in the carriage of passengers, cargo, or mail for remuneration or hire, it is considered revenue traffic; otherwise, it will be considered a nonrevenue traffic as it is non-remunerative.[2]

2.4 The Fourth Freedom: Freedom to Pick

The United Nations Economic and Social Council, (ECOSOC), in its decision relating to the implementation of the Yamoussoukro Declaration concerning the liberalization of access to air transport markets in Africa defines the fourth freedom as "the right of an Eligible Airline of one State party to take on, in the territory of another State party, passengers, freight and mail for offloading in the State party in which it is licensed."[3]

The fourth freedom enables scheduled international flight carriers to take on passengers, freights, and mails from a foreign State to a flag State. The third and fourth freedoms constitute the pillar of air carriage of passengers, mail, and cargo carried for remuneration or hire, commonly known as commercial flights, as the two freedoms allow to discharge and pick traffic.

An illustration can be found in Protocol 1 on unlimited third and fourth freedom traffic rights between any points in the contracting parties. The Protocol was signed between member states of the Association of Southern Asian Nations and provides in its Article 1 (1) that the designated airlines of each member state shall be allowed to operate scheduled air passenger and/or cargo services from any point in its territory with an international airport and vice versa.

As explained by Marc Dierikx, usually such freedoms are granted between States based on reciprocal rights.[4] The Bermuda agreement provides for such a practice.[5]

2.5 The Fifth Freedom: Freedom to Discharge and Take on between Two Different States

This freedom allows the carrier to make traffic between two different States outside the flag State. Such freedom is nevertheless subjected to a condition that the flight should have started and should end in the flag State. Alan Khee-Jin Tan explains that fifth freedoms are jealously guarded,[6] particularly where most States still apply rules of ownership and control of airlines.

There is a move to abandon restrictions for foreign ownership and control of airlines. Such a move might be supported by the current idea of liberalization of the airline industry; however, it should be indicated that the 1944 Chicago Convention was not negotiated during the era of globalization. The current trend might be departing from the initial idea, but the remnants of the old practice are still noticeable.

2.6 The Sixth Freedom: The Freedom of Traffic between Two Foreign States via the Flag State

Contrary to the previous five freedoms, which are *expressis verbis*, that is, subject to a written provision in various international treaties, the sixth freedom is usually not incorporated in many agreements. This freedom enables the airline to carry passengers, freight, and mail from one foreign State to another foreign State, but with a stop usually referred to as a connection in the flag State.[7]

Interestingly, the sixth freedom has been in application for a long time but it has not attracted enough attention. Technically, it can be understood as a combination of the third and fourth freedoms. Indeed, if an airline, through its flag State, has secured the third and fourth freedoms within two different countries, it might automatically exercise the sixth freedom without the existence of a written agreement on the sixth freedom.

The exercise of the sixth freedom will only depend upon the ability of the airline to collect traffic from various points to its hub, from which the airline will redistribute them to their various destinations. According to Hanlon, "The geographical locations of some airlines enable them to conduct operations, to exploit the large volumes of traffic which may be carried between foreign countries on through connecting services routed via their home states."[8]

2.7 The Seventh Freedom: The Freedom to Traffic between Two Points within a Foreign State

The seventh freedom enables a foreign international scheduled flight to directly carry traffic between two points within one State without having to make a stop in its flag State. It is important to note that when exercising the seventh freedom, the airline has no obligation to make such a flight part of a flight to or from its own home country by way of either connection or extension.

To put it differently, an airline may fly into another State, discharge and or take on traffic at two various points regardless of its origin and its destination, which does not have to be the flag State.

For instance, on February 05, 2020, the United States and Kenya signed an amendment to the US–Kenya Air Transport Agreement of December 04, 2019. The amendment allows US all-cargo airlines to fly between Kenya and a third nation without needing to stop in the United States. The same amendment gives Kenyan all-cargo carriers reciprocal rights to serve the United States.[9] Indeed, without saying it, the amendment adds a seventh freedom to the December 04, 2019 agreement.

2.8 The Eighth Freedom: Freedom to Cabotage

The *Max-Planck Encyclopedia of International Law* defines the concept of cabotage to mean "a commercial transportation service by a transportation company within a single country, i.e. between two points within the same country."[10] This applies when a scheduled international flight makes two traffics between two points that are located within a single State. However, such an international flight needs to have started or terminated in the flag State.

Interestingly, Article 7 of the 1944 Chicago Convention, providing for cabotage, stipulates that "each contracting State shall have the right to refuse permission to the aircraft of other contracting States to take on in its territory passengers, mail and cargo carried for remuneration or hire and destined for another point within its territory."

Indeed, the provision on the refusal of permission for international flights to cabotage is designed to discourage international airlines to get involved in domestic flights. However, if a given State is willing to grant to a given international airline the right to traffic locally, such authorization is equally accepted in air law, since it is considered as a matter of discretion of the granting State.

2.9 The Ninth Freedom: The Standalone Cabotage Freedom

The ninth freedom can be considered an extension of the eighth freedom as it removes the condition that the flight needs to originate or terminate in the flag State. Thus, the ninth freedom is considered pure cabotage or standalone cabotage.

This means that an international scheduled flight belonging to a given State can carry traffic between two points within a given State even when such a flight has started or will terminate in a third State, which is different from the flag State.

CHAPTER 3

Environmental Protection

Annex 16 of the 1944 Chicago Convention constitutes the main regulation as far as environmental protection from civil aviation's effects is concerned. Currently, the Annex is constituted of four volumes, of which volume one addresses the question of noise pollution, volume two is dedicated to aircraft engine emissions, volume three deals specifically with the question of aeroplane and CO_2 emissions, and volume four comprises two separate documents—the first addressing the question of Carbon Offsetting and Reduction Scheme for International Aviation (CORSIA), and the second being the Technical Manual, the procedure for demonstrating compliance with CORSIA.

This chapter will, therefore, discuss the two highlighted aspects—noise pollution and engine emissions—as it will try to understand the measures provided in the Annex for environmental protection.

3.1 Noise Pollution

Noise can be stressful to human beings. It can interrupt communication, disrupt sleep, negatively affect academic performance, cause detrimental cardiovascular effects,[1] which might cause hypertension, and so on.[2]

Indeed, medical evidence suggests that excessive noise can cause mental disorders and other detrimental psychological effects on human beings. It increases blood pressure and stress-related cholesterol levels; irritability and fatigue increase particularly when someone is exposed to excessive noise levels for several hours.[3]

Benedicte Claes's research has established that aircraft noise heard on the ground comes from three different sources. First, the noise is a mixture originating within the aircraft engines and those produced by the jet exhausts, where high-velocity gases are propelled into the atmospheric air, causing jet noise.[4] An additional source of noise occurs on the final approach to land, with the engines at low power and creating minimum noise. At that moment, aerodynamic disturbances caused by the deployment of the flaps and undercarriage produce a significant source of airframe noise.[5]

3.1.1 Regulatory Framework

As stated earlier, volume one of Annex 16 on environmental protection focuses on aircraft noise. The current seventh edition, adopted on March 03, 2014 during the ninth meeting of the Committee on Aviation Environment Protection (CAEP), finds its origins in the special meeting on aircraft noise in the vicinity of aerodromes of November–December 1969.[6]

The 1969 meeting was convened to examine the following questions:

a) Procedures for describing and measuring aircraft noise
b) Human tolerance to aircraft noise
c) Aircraft noise certification
d) Criteria for the establishment of aircraft noise abatement operating procedures

e)   Land-use control
f)   Ground run-up noise abatement procedures[7]

Thus, the ICAO Assembly in its thirty-third session resolved that the appendices attached to its resolution shall constitute the consolidated statement of continuing ICAO policies and practices related to environmental protection.

Appendix B recognized the magnitude of the problem of aircraft noise in the vicinity of many of the world's airports. The Appendix raises public concern as it highlights the limited airport infrastructure development. It emphasizes that appropriate action be taken considering that the future development of aviation could increase and aggravate the problems of aircraft noise and aircraft engine emissions.[8]

Appendix C acknowledges that the severity of the aircraft noise problem at many airports has given rise to measures that limit aircraft operations and has provoked vigorous opposition to the expansion of existing airports or construction of new airports. It states the following:

> The balanced approach to noise management developed by ICAO consists of identifying the noise problem at an airport and then analyzing the various measures available to reduce noise through the exploration of four principal elements, namely reduction at source, land-use planning and management, noise abatement operational procedures and operating restrictions, intending to address the noise problem most cost-effectively.[9]

It is in the spirit of finding various measures that could be resorted to in order to reduce noise pollution that ICAO has adopted the following noise certification requirements.

3.1.2 The Noise Certification Requirements

ICAO has the following three environmental goals for international aviation:

1) Reduce the number of people exposed to significant aircraft noise
2) Reduce the impact of aviation emissions on local air quality
3) Reduce the impact of aviation emissions on the global climate[10]

According to the ICAO Guidance on the Balanced Approach to Aircraft Noise Management, the balanced approach comprises four elements:

1) Noise reduction at the source
2) Land-use planning and management
3) Noise abatement operational procedures
4) Restrictions on operations[11]

As indicated in Appendix D of the Assembly Resolution A33-7, certification standards are specified in Volume I of Annex 16 (aircraft noise certification) as part of the strategy to reduce aircraft noise at the source.[12]

Part two of volume one contains the standard recommended practices and guidelines for noise certification applicable to the classification of aircrafts specified in each individual chapter of that part and applicable to aircrafts registered to engage in international flights.[13]

CAEP stated the following:

> The prime purpose of noise certification is to ensure that the latest available noise reduction technology is incorporated into the aircraft design demonstrated by procedures that are relevant to day-to-day operations, to ensure that noise reduction is offered by technology.[14]

Thus, reduction of noise is not limited to the development of new and more stringent standards or new, quieter aircraft types. It also results from constant technology improvement throughout the life cycle of an aircraft type. Such technology improvement should be progressively integrated into the system of manufacturing of new engines[15] thus improving its overall noise performance.[16]

This justifies why Annex 16 makes it mandatory for the State of Registry to issue or validate such a certificate upon satisfaction that the aircraft meets the requirements of Annex 16, particularly the requirements provided in chapter two.[17]

3.1.3 Land-Use Planning and Management

The number of people affected by aircraft noise is dependent on how the use of land surrounding an airport is planned and managed, in particular the extent to which residential development and other noise-sensitive activities are controlled.[18]

The objective of compatible land-use planning in this context is to direct incompatible land use such as schools, residential houses, and hospitals away from the airport environs and to encourage compatible use such as having industrial and commercial activities located around airport facilities.[19]

Noise zoning is, therefore, the exercise of the legal powers of the government that enables relevant authorities to designate various uses that are permitted for each parcel of land, depending on the noise exposure.

3.1.4 Noise Abatement Operational Procedures and Restrictions

The noise at the airport can be caused by in-flight aircraft but also by ground-based operational procedures. For instance, the departure procedure could be designed to optimize the distribution to the exposure of noise at a particular location on the ground.[20]

While the continuous descent approach could allow an inter-rupted descent from cruising altitude, usually referred to as descent with no segment of level flight exceeding 2 or 2.5 NM, it also reduces the noise experienced on the ground by reducing the overall thrust required during initial descent and keeping the aircraft higher for longer.[21]

While operating restrictions are designed to limit or prohibit movements of the noisiest aircraft at an airport, enabling the airport to contain or shrink the noise contour around the airport, the ICAO Assembly urges States not to permit the introduction of any operating restriction aimed at the withdrawal of aircraft that comply through either original certification or recertification with noise standards in volume one, chapter four of Annex 16.

3.2 The Carbon Dioxide Emission

3.2.1 The Problem

In September 2019, the *Guardian* reported that "carbon dioxide emitted by commercial flights rose by 32% from 2013 to 2018."[22] Indeed, the newspaper indicated that worldwide CO_2 emissions from commercial flights was rising up to 70 percent faster than predicted by the UN.[23] During the coronavirus pandemic, as aviation was paralyzed, the CO_2 emissions declined considerably. However, the post–COVID-19 world has seen a resumption of the rising emission of CO_2.[24]

Despite a significant improvement in the efficiency of aircraft and flight operations over the last 60 years,[25] the growing aviation sector is expected to experience a threefold increase between 2000 and 2050 in terms of passengers,[26] which might have the same impact on the degradation of the environment.

If aviation has thus far produced between 2 and 3 percent of total CO_2 emissions,[27] which might be considered a relatively small percentage of pollution, as explained by Professor Dempsey, this is the only industry that discharges harmful emissions directly into the upper atmosphere, thus contributing more profoundly to global warming and ozone depletion.[28] Indeed, this is a non-negligible factor considering the rate of growth of the aviation industry.[29]

Pollutants emitted into the atmosphere by aviation might be a factor contributing to global warming. Professor Lee suggests, "The principal greenhouse gas pollutant emitted from aviation is CO_2 (carbon dioxide). Other emissions from aviation that affect the radioactive balance include nitrogen oxides (NOx, where $NO_x = NO + NO_2$), sulfate and soot particles, and water vapor, which lead to a variety of effects."[30] The same researcher indicates that the total cumulative CO_2 emissions have a relationship with the temperature response of the earth-atmosphere system.[31]

This explains why ICAO Annex 16, in its volume II—Aircraft Engine Emission—aims at limiting aircraft emissions by way of engine certification. Indeed, the Annex indicates that the gas concentration of the following emissions shall be determined:

a) Hydrocarbon (HC)
b) Carbon monoxide (CO)
c) Carbon dioxide (CO_2)
d) Oxide of Nitrogen (NO_x)
e) Nitric Oxide (NO)[32]

Whereas in its volume II which discusses certification standards, the Annex stipulates that "CO_2 emission certification shall be granted or validated by the State of Registry of an aeroplane on the basis of satisfactory evidence that the aeroplane complies with requirements that are least equal to the applicable standards specified in this Annex."

3.2.2 Regulatory Framework

Annex 16 might look recent with its latest edition being dated of 2018. However, ICAO's efforts to address the question of environmental protection could be traced back to the early 1970s. Indeed, ICAO Council adopted its first standards and recommendations for environmental protection on April 02, 1971.

The Council had acted according to the provision of Article 37 of the 1944 Chicago Convention:

> Each contracting State undertakes to collaborate in securing the highest practicable degree of uniformity in regulations, standards, procedures, and organization concerning aircraft, personnel, airways, and auxiliary services in all matters in which such uniformity will facilitate and improve air navigation.

The Article might not provide specifically for environmental protection, but since the issue requires uniformity in regulation and application, nothing would prevent this legislation from being considered as a legal basis for this Annex.

Thus, in 1972, the United Nations Conference on Human Environment was held in Stockholm and was attended by ICAO delegates. It recommended that an intergovernmental body for environmental affairs be established within the United Nations. Such a body was given the assignment to conduct surveys on the need and possibilities of developing internationally agreed standards for measuring and limiting noise emissions and that, if it is deemed advisable, such standards shall be applied in the production of means of transportation and certain kinds of working.[33]

In the following ICAO Assembly, the Council was requested to continue, with the assistance and cooperation of other bodies of the organization together with other international organizations. The main task was to continue to develop the standards, recommended practices and procedures, and/or guidance material dealing with the quality of the human environment.[34]

In 1977, the ICAO issued Circular 134 on the Control of Aircraft Engine Emissions. The Circular contains guidance in the form of a certification procedure for the control of vented fuel, smoke, and certain gaseous emissions for new turbojet and turbofan engines intended for propulsion at subsonic speeds.

3.2.3 Emission Certificate Requirement

In its part 3, volume 2, Annex 16 addresses the question of emissions certificate. Indeed, it provides that an emission certificate shall be granted by the certificating authority based on satisfactory evidence that the engine complies with requirements that are at least equal to the stringency of volume 2 of Annex 16.[35]

The volume provides guidelines to test the engine emission before the issuance of the required certificate. It provides for test procedures and calculations of emissions. Despite having stringent measures, the system accommodates a certain level of flexibility in the sense that, if an engine type would fail the test, the certifying authority would allow the manufacturer to conduct additional tests, as they are equally allowed to make an engine modification until compliance will be demonstrated. However, if such compliance is not demonstrated, the engine type will have to be withdrawn.[36]

It could be concluded that Annex 16, volume II calls for the prevention of intentional fuel venting and establishes standards for aircraft emissions control through an engine certification scheme. Fuel venting occurs when a plane has been designed in such a manner that the fuel nozzle manifolds discharge liquid fuel during normal flight or ground operations.

CHAPTER 4

Security of Aircraft

4.1 The Problem

The concept of aviation security needs to be distinguished from the concept of safety in aviation. Whereas safety refers to the design, manufacture, maintenance, and operation of aircraft, aviation security refers to malicious acts against aircraft and their passengers and crew.[1] Thus, the problem raised by security in the aviation industry is understood as a combination of measures and human and material resources intended to protect international civil aviation against acts of unlawful interference.[2]

The threat to the security of aircraft has existed throughout the history of air navigation. A wide range of motives have been identified behind such threats. As explained by Brian A. Jackson and David R. Frelinger, such motives would vary from individuals seeking transport, the setting up of hostages, an act of sabotage, to full-scale terrorist attacks of the magnitude of the September 11th, 2001, Al-Qaida attack in the United States.[3]

Indeed, these attacks triggered quick responses from various quarters, including the ICAO Assembly, which, to ensure the safety, security, and efficiency of flights worldwide, "directed the Council to seek ways to shorten the process for the approval and adoption of SARPs considered of key importance for the safety and security of civil aviation."[4] In Europe, the European Council

Regulation (EC) No 2320/2002[5] was quickly adopted in 2002 by the European Parliament and the Council to address the question of civil aviation security.

Although the September 11th terrorist attacks changed the world's perception of the security of aircraft, it should be noted that such attacks have existed before and that the international community had responded to them with various legal measures, as discussed here.

4.2 Evolution of the Law

4.2.1 The 1963 Tokyo Convention on Offenses and Certain Other Acts Committed on Board Aircraft

The increase in the number of aircraft highjacked in the early 1960s was one of the reasons that led to the adoption of the 1963 Tokyo Convention on offenses and certain other acts committed on board aircraft.[6] Already, Article 1 of the 1963 Tokyo Convention provides that it will apply in respect of offenses against penal law and acts that, whether or not are criminal offenses, may or do jeopardize the safety of the aircraft or of persons or property therein, or that jeopardize good order and discipline on board.[7]

The Convention gives jurisdiction over such offenses and acts committed on board to the State of registration.[8] However, any other State may have jurisdiction over the case when the committed offense has effect on the territory of another State, or when the offense has been committed by or against a national or permanent resident of another State, when the offense has been committed against the security of another State, when the offense consists of a breach of any rule or regulations relating to the flight or maneuver of aircraft in force in such State, or the exercise of jurisdiction is necessary to ensure the observance of any obligation of such State under a multilateral agreement.[9]

Furthermore, if the aircraft commander has reasonable ground to believe that a person has committed, or is about to commit, on board the aircraft, an offense or act contemplated in Article 1, paragraph 1, they may impose reasonable measures against such a person, including restraints that are necessary to protect the safety of the aircraft.[10]

Such measures of restraint imposed on such a person end at any point where the aircraft lands. However, if the aircraft lands in a non-contracting State and the local authorities refuse to permit disembarkation of that person or if the aircraft makes a forced landing and the aircraft commander is unable to deliver that person to competent authorities or if the person concerned agrees to onward carriage under restraint, such measures would remain in application until such a time that the aircraft will land in the flag State or in any other State willing to carry out legal proceedings with respect to that person.[11]

The Convention provides that when a person on board has unlawfully committed, by force or threat thereof, an act of interference, seizure, or other wrongful exercises of control of an aircraft in flight or when such an act is about to be committed, contracting States shall take all appropriate measures to restore control of the aircraft to its lawful commander or to preserve his control of the aircraft.[12]

The Convention can be given the merit of recognizing that, other than acts considered offenses by the penal law, there are other acts that may jeopardize the safety of the aircraft good order and discipline on board. It further has given powers to the commander to take measures against a given suspect. However, it does not define how the act can jeopardize the safety of the aircraft, nor does it have any provisions on the process other than handing the suspect over to the State concerned, which will address the matter according to its legislation.

4.2.2 The 1970 Hague Convention for Suppression of Unlawful Seizure of Aircraft

The 1970 Hague Convention stresses how unlawful acts of seizure and exercise of control of an aircraft in flight could jeopardize the safety of onboard passengers and properties. Such seizure affects the operations of the air services and undermines the confidence of travelers in the safety of civil aviation, which the Convention considers a matter of serious concern.[13]

Article 1 of the Convention defines such crime as the fact that a person unlawfully, that is, by force or by the threat of force, or by any other form of intimidation, seizes, or exercises control of an aircraft, or attempts to perform any of the aforementioned acts.[14]

The Convention further establishes the jurisdiction of the State of registration when the offense is committed on board an aircraft registered in that State, when the aircraft on board of which the offense is committed lands in its territory with the alleged offender still on board, or when the offense is committed on board of such aircraft leased without crew to a lessee who has his principal place of business or, if the lessee has no such place of business, his permanent residence in that State.[15]

Its innovative Article 7 provides that the contracting State in the territory of which the alleged offender is found shall, if it does not extradite him, be obliged, without exception whatsoever and whether or not the offense was committed in its territory, to submit the case to its competent authorities for prosecution. Article 8 encourages State parties to include the offense as an extraditable offense in every extradition treaty to be concluded between them.

The application of Article 8 (2), according to which, if a contracting State that makes extradition conditional on the existence of a treaty receives a request for extradition from another contracting State with which it has no extradition treaty, it may consider this Convention as the legal basis for extradition in respect of the offense.[16] Nevertheless, no derogatory powers should be given to the extradition law.

4.2.3 The 1971 Montreal Convention for Suppression of Unlawful Acts against the Safety of Civil Aviation

Article 1 (1) of the 1971 Montreal Convention provides that a person commits an unlawful act if such a person performs an act of violence against a person on board an aircraft in flight, if that act is likely to endanger the safety of that aircraft, or if such a person destroys an aircraft in service or causes damage to such an aircraft that renders it incapable of flight or that is likely to endanger its safety in flight.[17]

The Article provides that a person commits an unlawful act if such a person places or causes to be placed on an aircraft in service, by any means whatsoever, a device or substance that is likely to destroy that aircraft or cause damage to the aircraft that renders it incapable of flight or cause damage to the aircraft that is likely to endanger its safety in flight, or destroys or damages air navigation facilities or interferes with their operation, if any such act is likely to endanger the safety of aircraft in flight.[18]

Article 5 creates an obligation for States parties to take measures to establish their jurisdiction over the aforementioned unlawful acts, particularly when the offense is committed in the territory of that State or when the offense is committed against or on board an aircraft registered in that State. The same will apply when the aircraft on board which the offense is committed lands in its territory with the alleged offender still on board or when the offense is committed against or on board an aircraft leased without crew to a lessee who has his principal place of business or, if the lessee has no such place of business, his permanent residence in that State.

Article 7 creates an obligation *out dedere out judicare*, that is, each contracting State in the territory of which the alleged offender is found, shall, if it does not extradite him, be obliged to submit the case to its competent authorities for legal prosecution.

The 1971 Montreal Convention is supplemented by the 1988 Montreal Protocol for the Suppression of Unlawful Acts of Violence at Airports Serving International Civil Aviation.

The Protocol adds the following new paragraph to Article 1 of the Convention:

> Any person commits an offense if he unlawfully and intentionally uses any device, substance, or weapon: performs an act of violence against a person at an airport serving international civil aviation which causes or is likely to cause serious injury or death or destroys or seriously damages the facilities of an airport serving international civil aviation or aircraft not in service located thereon or disrupts the services of the airport if such an act endangers or is likely to endanger safety at the airport.

4.2.4 The 1991 Montreal Convention on the Marking of Plastic Explosive for the Purposes of Detection

The bombing of Pan Am flight 103 over Lockerbie, Scotland, on December 21, 1988 might have influenced the adoption of the 1991 Montreal Convention, which finds its sources in the United Nations Security Council Resolution 635 of 14 June 1989. The Resolution urged ICAO to intensify its work aimed at preventing all acts of terrorism against international civil aviation, in particular its work on devising an international regime for the marking of plastic or sheet explosives for the purpose of detection.

The Technical Annex defines explosives as formulated with one or more high explosives that, in their pure form, have a vapor pressure less than 10^{-4} Pa at a temperature of $25°C$ *and* defines high explosives to include cyclotetramethylenetetranitramine (HMX) as it explodes at high temperatures. Indeed HMX is usually used in the making of explosives, rocket fuels, and buster chargers.

The same Annex includes pentaerythritol tetranitrate (PETN), which is known for its explosive properties, particularly when mixed with a plasticizer. The Technical Annex also refers to cyclotrimethylenetrinitramine (RDX), which is a highly explosive white powder.[19]

The 1991 Montreal Convention stipulates that each State party shall take necessary measures to exercise strict and effective control over the possession and transfer of possession of unmarked explosives either manufactured or brought into its territory. States parties are equally under the duty to take necessary measures to ensure that all stocks of those explosives that are not held by its official authorities are destroyed.[20]

The purpose of the Convention is to ensure that such explosives, either in their final state or in the processing state, are not held by any individual but rather by States.

4.3 The Annexes

4.3.1 Annex 17

Other than the various conventions that have addressed the question of unlawful interference, as discussed earlier, the annexes to the 1944 Chicago Convention have also addressed the matter.

Annex 17 to the 1944 Chicago Convention on International Civil Aviation is dedicated to the security and safeguarding of international civil aviation against acts of unlawful interference and defines acts of unlawful interference as acts or attempted acts to jeopardize the safety of civil aviation.

Such acts include unlawful seizure of aircraft; destruction of an aircraft in service; hostage taking on board aircraft or on aerodromes; forcible intrusion on board an aircraft, at an airport or on the premises of an aeronautical facility; introduction on board an aircraft or at an airport of a weapon or hazardous device or material intended for criminal purposes; use of an aircraft in service to cause death, serious bodily injury, or serious damage to property or the environment; and communication of false information so as to jeopardize the safety of an aircraft in flight or on the ground, of passengers, crew, ground personnel, or the general public, at an airport or on the premises of a civil aviation facility.[21]

It is important to note that Annex 17, alongside the ICAO SARPs relating to aviation security, does not create binding norms of international law but rather recommendations calling upon States to establish regulations on civil aviation security meeting the required standard[22] and ensure that airlines operating within their territories do comply with such regulations,[23] as will be discussed later.

As far as preventive measures are concerned, chapter four of the Annex requires States to establish measures to prevent weapons, explosives, or any other dangerous devices, articles, or substances that may be used to commit an act of unlawful interference, the carriage or bearing of which is not authorized, from being introduced, by any means whatsoever, on board an aircraft engaged in civil aviation.[24]

Furthermore, whenever there will be reliable information that an aircraft may be subjected to an act of unlawful interference, the State shall take measures to safeguard the aircraft, including search for possible hidden weapons if the aircraft is still on the ground. If such aircraft has already departed, the State shall notify relevant authorities at the landing airport.[25] Such notification may include all important flight information.

Each contracting State in which an aircraft subjected to an act of unlawful interference has landed shall notify by the most expeditious means the State of Registry of the aircraft and the State of the Operator of the landing and shall similarly transmit by the most expeditious means all other relevant information to each State whose citizens have been affected by such interference, such as the States whose citizens have suffered fatalities or injuries or were detained as hostages or are known to have been on board the aircraft. The same information shall be sent to the ICAO.[26]

4.3.2 Annex 11

Other than Annex 17, other annexes too have provisions relevant to the security of aircraft. This is the case for Annex 11, which is focused on Air Traffic Control. However, in Chapter 2, the Annex provides that an aircraft known or believed to be in a state of emergency, including being subjected to unlawful interference, shall be given maximum consideration, assistance, and priority over other aircrafts as may be necessitated by the circumstances.[27]

It is innovative that the Annex suggests that aircraft be equipped with appropriate data link capability and/or a secondary surveillance radar (SSR) transponder might operate the equipment on Mode A Code 7700 or on Mode A Code 7500.[28]

Code 7700 is designed to provide recognition of an aircraft in an emergency, whereas Code 7500 provides recognition of an aircraft that is being subjected to unlawful interference. An aircraft equipped with an SSR transponder is expected to operate the transponder on Mode A Code 7500 to indicate specifically that it is the subject of unlawful interference. The aircraft may operate the transponder on Mode A Code 7700 to indicate that it is threatened by grave and imminent danger and requires immediate assistance.

CHAPTER 5

Air Traffic   ontrol Service (ATCS)

The history of ATCS could be traced back to 1929, when Archie William League, considered the first air traffic controller, was hired by St. Louis Lambert International Airport in the United States. He operated his control tower from a wheelbarrow and would raise his checkered flag to signal to the pilot to proceed or would raise the red flag to indicate to the pilot not to proceed with the next maneuver, that is, they should remain in the same position where they were until he clears them to engage in the next move.[1]

According to Annex 11 of the 1944 Chicago Convention, ATCS is understood as a service provided to prevent collisions either between aircrafts or, in the maneuvering area, between an aircraft and obstructions.[2] The same is used to facilitate the flow of air traffic expeditiously, as it provides useful information to ensure efficient coordination of flights when they are taking off, en route, in distress, or landing.[3]

5.1 Air Traffic Management

To enable the ATC to discharge its duties, it shall be provided with all information on every aircraft trajectory projection within its jurisdiction and any subsequent change thereafter. Indeed, even with such information, it is important to note that factors such as wind gusts or navigational error might have repercussions on the accuracy of the trajectory projection.[4]

It is based on the information received from all the aircrafts within its area that the ATC shall determine the position of all known aircrafts from each other at any given time before it expeditiously clears them to proceed with their traffic.[5]

In the event of a conflict of traffic, that is, when two or more aircraft lose the minimum separation between them,[6] the Air Traffic Service, (ATS) shall separate such aircrafts by doing at least one of the following:

    a)   Vertical separation, obtained by assigning different levels selected from
        1) the appropriate table of cruising levels or
        2) a modified table of cruising levels.
    b)   Horizontal separation, obtained by providing
        1) longitudinal separation, by maintaining an interval between aircraft operating along the same, converging, or reciprocal tracks, expressed in time or distance, or
        2) lateral separation, by maintaining aircraft on different routes or in different geographical areas.[7]

It is equally possible to separate two aircrafts by a combination of a vertical separation with either a longitudinal separation or a lateral separation. Indeed, the ATC aims to generate a conflict-free trajectory soon after such potential conflict is noticed.[8]

5.2 Delineation of the ATCS Territorial Jurisdiction

Given the fact that the airspace above a national territory, including its territorial waters, belongs to the State controlling the territory, it is upon that State to determine which part of their territory, or rather which part of their airspace, will be covered by their air traffic services.

No State is under any obligation to provide air traffic services for its entire airspace. The establishment of such services is dictated by the structure of the air routing, coupled with the need to provide efficient services, considering every State's capacity.

Furthermore, a State may delegate its duty to provide air traffic services in its airspace to another State.[9] Such agreement does not translate into the transfer of any sovereign right of such a State. The delegating State remains the sole authority over its airspace, although that it has delegated the exercise of its duty to establish air traffic services to another State, which usually will entrust such duty to its ATCS to exercise such duties on its behalf. It should be indicated that these types of agreements fall under the bilateral technical cooperation between States and are regulated by public international law.

The provision of air traffic services in the airspace above the high seas, where necessary, is determined by a multilateral air navigation treaty. In most cases, such a treaty is negotiated within the framework of regional organizations, if possible. Indeed, such treaties will assign the duty of provision of such services to a given State or will subdivide portions of the area concerned between different States, based on whichever formula is efficient, on a case-by-case basis.

5.3 Cooperation with Meteorological Services

Considering the importance of meteorological information both before the flight, as part of the pre-flight information, and during it, as the timely update that usually is relayed to pilots as part of their in-flight information, air traffic services must establish constant and efficient cooperation between themselves and the meteorological services.

Annex 11 provides the following:

Arrangements shall be made between aeronautical information services and air traffic services authorities responsible for air traffic services to report to the responsible aeronautical information services unit, with a minimum of delay:

a)   information on aerodrome conditions;
b)   the operational status of associated facilities, services, and navigation aids within their area of responsibility;
c)   the occurrence of volcanic activity observed by air traffic services personnel or reported by aircraft; and
d)   any other information considered to be of operational significance.[10]

Thus, there is a duty of cooperation not just between the air traffic controller and the aircraft under their control, but such cooperation is also extended to the authority in charge of meteorological services, as it is equally extended to other traffic controllers.

5.4 The One Controller at Time Rule

Much that one ATC is in charge of many aircrafts at a time, as one controller would indeed control all aircrafts within its controlled airspace unless the ATC has delegated control of a certain area or certain aircrafts to one of its units, the one controller at a time rule rather means that one aircraft shall be all the time under the exclusive control of one controller at any given time. To put it differently, the responsibility for the control of all aircraft operating within a given airspace shall be vested in a single ATC unit, although the control of an aircraft or groups of aircraft may be delegated to another ATC unit.[11]

Thus, when an aircraft is moving toward entering a given airspace controlled by a different ATC, the responsibility for control of the flight is transferred by a clearance from the previous ATC to the other. Annex 11 provides that such transfer shall indicate

a) aircraft identification as shown in the flight plan;
b) clearance limit;
c) route of flight;
d) level(s) of flight for the entire route or part thereof and changes of levels if required; and
e) any necessary instructions or information on other matters such as approach or departure maneuvers, communications, and the time of expiry of the clearance.[12]

5.5 Strayed Aircraft

The aviation dictionary defines a strayed aircraft as "an aircraft that has deviated significantly from its intended track or which reports that it is lost."[13] The same dictionary indicates that, to a certain extent, an unidentified aircraft may be considered a strayed aircraft when such an aircraft is observed or reported to be operating in a given area when its identity has not been established.[14]

Any Air Traffic Control that notices a strayed aircraft or an aircraft that is about to go astray is under the duty to assist such aircraft. Such assistance is particularly important when the area where the aircraft is located or where it is heading is an area of risk of interception or other hazardous areas to the safety of the aircraft.[15]

According to the Civil Aviation Authority, a stray VFR, meaning flights conducted in accordance with visual flight rules, is to be considered in a state of emergency and handled as such. The ATC shall request any of the following information to be able to assist the pilot:

a) Aircraft flight conditions
b) Position (if known) and flight level/altitude
c) Airspeed and heading since last known position, if pertinent
d) Pilot experience
e) Navigation equipment carried and if any navigation aid signals are being received
f) SSR Mode and code selected if relevant
g) Departure and destination aerodromes
h) Number of persons on board
i) Fuel endurance[16]

Although VFR flights are more exposed to getting lost, even IFR, meaning flights conducted in accordance with instrument flight rules, are not immune from such incidences.

In the event that an Air Traffic Control (ATC) has not yet established contact with a given strayed aircraft but is aware that such aircraft position is not known, Annex 11 advises that the Air Traffic Service(ATS) shall

a) attempt to establish two-way communication with the aircraft, unless such communication already exists;
b) use all available means to determine its position;
c) inform other ATS units into whose area the aircraft may have strayed or may stray, taking into account all the factors that may have affected the navigation of the aircraft in the circumstances; and
d) inform, following the locally agreed procedures, appropriate military units and provide them with pertinent flight plans and other data concerning strayed aircraft[17]

Furthermore, the ATS shall request assistance from other in-flight aircraft in establishing communication with the strayed aircraft and determining its position.

Once the position of the strayed aircraft is known to an ATC and communication with the aircraft becomes established, the ATCS shall eventually inform the aircraft of its coordinates as well as direct it toward its correct route.

The ATS shall equally inform other ATS and appropriate military units of the whereabouts of the strayed aircraft and any subsequent directives given to it in an attempt to return it either to its initial route or toward the nearest airport, as the case may be.

In the event that an ATS notices an unidentified aircraft, it has to attempt to identify such aircraft. Accordingly, Annex 11 indicates that the ATC shall

a) attempt to establish two-way communication with the aircraft;

b) inquire of other ATS units within the flight information region about the flight and request their assistance in establishing two-way communication with the aircraft; and

c) attempt to obtain information from other aircraft in the area.[18]

Once the identity of such aircraft has been established, the ATS shall inform the appropriate military authorities of the identity of such aircraft and its trajectory. It is always advised to either direct the strayed aircraft toward its normal trajectory or the nearest airport.

CHAPTER 6

Aircraft Search and Rescue

The concept of aircraft search means an operation coordinated by a rescue center to locate an aircraft in distress,[1] whereas the concept of rescue will apply when the operation is to retrieve persons in distress, provide for their initial medical or other needs, and deliver them to a place of safety.[2] Indeed, the operation of search and rescue comprises the search for the aircraft and the provision of aid to persons therein who might be in imminent danger.

Usually, the search is initiated when there is a situation whereby there is reasonable certainty that an aircraft and its occupants are threatened by grave and imminent danger and require immediate assistance. That means the call for search and rescue has reached the level of distress.[3]

Such a phase comes after the alert phase, at which level there is an apprehension. In other words, there exists some anxiety or fear for the safety of an aircraft and its occupants. As the name indicates, in this phase, the search and rescue units are on alert, meaning that all the search plans for the search operation are made to initiate the search process.

To put it differently, the alert phase exists when an aircraft or persons on board such aircraft are having some difficulty and may need assistance, but are not in immediate danger. There might be some fear about the safety of the aircraft and passengers on board; however, no known threat requires immediate action.

This phase should not be confused with the uncertainty phase, which is a lower level in the sense that the search and rescue units are rather gathering all necessary information and reports to assess the situation and decide on the subsequent strategy.

The Australian National Search and Rescue Manual defines the concept by highlighting the fact that "the uncertainty phase is assigned any time doubt/uncertainty exists as to the safety of an aircraft, vessel or person because of knowledge of possible difficulties, or because of lack of information concerning progress or position."[4]

Indeed, if an aircraft is generally in such conditions that its progress must be constantly monitored due to either the geographical position of its location or a change of weather or any factor that might endanger its safety at any time, that information needs to be communicated to the pilot, although the state of its danger does not yet warrant the dispatching of a search and rescue mission.

If such information is generally not provided for more than 15 minutes from the time it was expected or the aircraft does not report at a given position it should have been reported to be at a given time, even though there might not be a formal request for assistance to such aircraft, all factors taken into consideration, there is fear or doubt that such aircraft could be in distress. Indeed, there is uncertainty concerning such aircraft, and such a situation can be expected to escalate.

6.1 Regulatory Framework

Article 25 of the 1944 Chicago Convention provides the following:

> Each Contracting State undertakes to provide such measures
> of assistance to aircraft in distress in its territory as it may find

practicable, and to permit, subject to control by its authorities, the owners of aircraft or authorities of the State in which the aircraft is registered to provide such measures of assistance as may be necessitated by the circumstances. Each Contracting State, when undertaking a search for missing aircraft, will collaborate in coordinated measures which may be recommended from time to time pursuant to this Convention.

To materialize this Article, Annex 12 to the Convention was dedicated to the search and rescue of missing aircraft and constitutes part of the legal framework relevant to search and rescue.

In addition, various countries have developed their manuals and legislations, which serve as guidelines for their search and rescue agencies.

6.2 The Search Operation

If the search and rescue unit does not have any information on the location of the aircraft, its position can be ascertained by estimating the possible area to be searched according to the position it was last located in, combined with the direction of its routing according to its intended destination. Considering the particularity of each search and rescue operation, such determination should provide for an allowance of a certain margin of error in its estimates.

If such an area is located within the search zone of an already established standby search and rescue zone of a given unit, such unit shall have the first responsibility to initiate the search and rescue mission. If the possible position of the aircraft is unknown, usually the search and rescue units shall search within their respective zones in consultation with adjacent search and rescue units along the route of the aircraft.

Ruwantissa Abeyratne suggests that, if any search and rescue regions extend over the territories of two or more States, or parts thereof, agreement thereon should be negotiated between the States concerned. Otherwise, an agreement between all the parties concerned might be set up to solve the relevant question of a joint search.[5]

It is advisable that any search and rescue plan should take into consideration all its strengths and constraints, including the size of the area to be searched, the capacity of the search units, the accessibility of the search zone, and weather conditions.

6.3 The Datum (Point de Repère)

As indicated in the Canadian National Search and Rescue Manual, the datum is the starting point of reference for any search and rescue operation; it is the establishment of the last known position of the aircraft.[6]

Considering that there might be a possibility of post-distress survivor motion, the datum must be adjusted to accommodate such margin; thus, the datum could be a geographic point, a line, or a given area used as a reference in search planning.[7]

When the distress position is not precisely known, the intended route of the aircraft is usually considered the first area for search.

6.4 The Possibility Area

The possibility area is the area where the aircraft is most likely to be found. Such an area is delineated by drawing a circle from the last known position. Considering that the aircraft could proceed in any direction until it exhausts its fuel, the radius of such a circle should be equal to the endurance of the aircraft from its last known point to the point of fuel exhaustion.

Thus, as indicated in the Australian manual, the possibility area may be determined by drawing a wind vector downwind from the last known position to a scale representing a distance equal to the wind speed multiplied by the estimated remaining fuel endurance time and by drawing a circle from the end of the wind vector, of a radius representing a distance equal to the aircraft true airspeed multiplied by estimated remaining fuel endurance.[8]

True airspeed needs to be taken into consideration because at 10,000 feet, true airspeed is usually faster than the airspeed indicator. Indeed, true airspeed is the speed of the aircraft relative to the air it is flying through. As the aircraft climbs higher, its surrounding pressure decreases as there will be fewer molecules in the air as its true airspeed increases.[9] It is estimated that, for every thousand feet above sea level, true airspeed is about 2 percent higher than the indicated airspeed.[10]

6.5 The Rescue Procedure

As soon as the missing aircraft is seen, the search and rescue unit must immediately report this to the search and rescue center. The search and rescue unit should proceed by providing all possible identification; if no identification can be done, the search and rescue unit shall make an indication in that respect.

The search and rescue unit needs to use all possible means to let the searched aircraft take notice that it has been sighted and remain within the visibility of the search and rescue unit. This is done to ensure the psychological well-being of the crew and passengers.

If the search crew is unable to rescue, the search unit shall scrutinize the area for further rescue and investigations. It would be advisable to take photographic images of the accident area and its surrounding area.[11]

For the sake of accident investigation, the accident site must be guarded, as disturbance of pieces of wreckage must be avoided except when necessary for the purpose of evacuation of survivors or their remaining

In the unfortunate event that after the search area has been covered and the search and rescue center considers that there might not be any likelihood that any survivor will be recovered, the search operation may be downscaled. However, there is an obligation of notification to the next of kin of such a decision. Considering the implications of such a decision, it is usually subjected to a certain procedure of approval by various authorities.

At a point when it becomes obvious that any prolonged search will constitute a waste of resources that could be used to rescue any other possible aircraft in the future, it is advisable that the relevant authorities, once satisfied, authorize the reduction of the search.

The concept of search reduction shall be understood to mean that, although the search is still open, as the missing aircraft has not been found, no further search activities are planned when all leads have been exhausted.[12]

Nevertheless, even after the reduction of the search has been formally approved, if new evidence suggests a strong likelihood of locating survivors, nothing shall prevent the planning of further search. However, considering that, as time passes, the likelihood of finding survivors becomes thin, it is nevertheless acceptable that if the circumstances of a particular case so require, such a possibility remains an option.

Usually changes in climatic conditions that might make the wreckage more visible at a later date would not constitute grounds for reopening a general search, since if there was any hope of discovering survivors, the search would not have been reduced.[13]

CHAPTER 7

Rules of the Air

Article 12 of the 1944 Chicago Convention, which provides for the Rules of the Air, creates an obligation upon each State party to adopt measures that will ensure that every aircraft flying over or maneuvering within its territory or every aircraft carrying its nationality mark, wherever such aircraft may be, shall comply with the rules and regulations relating to the flight and maneuver of aircraft in force.

However, States are under obligation to comply with the uniformity requirement to the greatest possible extent as they are expected to set up rules and regulations in conformity with the 1944 Chicago Convention and its Annexes. The Convention further stipulates that it will be of application to any aircraft overflying the high seas.[1]

7.1 Application of Rules of State of Registration

When not overflying the high seas, the aircraft may apply the rules of the air of the State of its registration as long as they are not conflicting with the rules of the air of the State being overflown.[2]

Otherwise, Annex 2 provides that the operation of an aircraft, either in flight or on the movement area of an aerodrome, shall comply with the general rules when in flight, that is, either VFR or IFR.[3]

7.2 Prohibition of the Use of Psychoactive Substances

The World Health Organization defines the concept of psychoactive substances as such substances that, when taken in or administered into one's system, affect mental processes, for example, perception, consciousness, cognition, mood, and emotions.[4]

In international law there are three main conventions controlling drugs and narcotics: the 1961 Single Convention on Narcotic Drugs as amended by the 1972 Protocol, the 1971 Convention on Psychotropic Substances, and the 1988 Convention Against Illicit Traffic in Narcotic Drugs and Psychotropic Substances.

Article 1(n) of the 1988 Convention stipulates that narcotic drug means any of the substances, natural or synthetic, in Schedules I and II of the Single Convention on Narcotic Drugs, 1961 as amended by the 1972 Protocol.

Although it is understood that substances like opium poppy, coca bush, and cannabis plants are not considered as falling within the definition of drugs as per the 1988 Convention, they are defined in Article 14(2) as plants containing narcotics or psychotropic substances.[5] The opium poppy is of particular interest to us, considering that it is a plant of the species papaver somniferum.

Further, Article 1 (r) defines psychotropic substance as any substance, natural or synthetic, or any natural material in Schedules I, II, III, and IV of the Convention on Psychotropic Substances, 1971. An updated table of the drugs and psychotropic substances is provided by the UN document ST/CND/1/Add.3/Rev5.[6]

In air law, no person whose function is critical to the safety of aviation, otherwise called safety-sensitive personnel, shall undertake that function while under the influence of any psychoactive substance because of which human performance is impaired. No such person shall engage in any kind of problematic use of substances.[7]

7.3 Right of Way Rules

The right of way rule is designed to help two aircrafts flying in each other's proximity to know which one has the right of the way, thus preventing collision as they approach each other. Various scenarios can be imagined, for instance, when one aircraft is approaching the other from the rear, when two aircraft are approaching each other head-on, or when the two aircraft are converging, overtaking, or landing.

As a matter of rule, when an aircraft has the right of way, it shall maintain its heading and speed, whereas the other aircraft should keep out of the way and shall avoid passing over, under, or in front of that aircraft.[8] Such passage can nevertheless be allowed if it has been cleared before the passing of the aircraft that has the right of the way, that is, such aircraft will have passed but it will equally cause no turbulences to the other aircraft.

This is the case when two aircrafts are converging. As Annex 2 puts it:

When two aircrafts are converging at approximately the same level, the aircraft that has the other on its right shall give way, except as follows:

a)   Power-driven, heavier-than-air aircraft shall give way to airships, gliders, and balloons.

b) Airships shall give way to gliders and balloons.
c) Gliders shall give way to balloons.
d) Power-driven aircraft shall give way to aircraft that are seen to be towing other aircraft or objects.[9]

When two aircraft are approaching one another head-on, neither of them has the right of way. Each aircraft will alter its heading to the right to avoid the collision.[10] However, when an aircraft is approaching from the rear, that is, when the aircraft is overtaking another aircraft on a line forming an angle less than 70 degrees with the plane of symmetry of the latter, the aircraft that is being overtaken has the right of way, meaning the overtaking aircraft shall keep out of the way of the other aircraft by altering its heading to the right.[11]

When landing or when operating on the ground or on water, the aircraft in flight shall give way to the aircraft landing. When two or more aircraft are approaching the airport for landing, the aircraft at the higher level shall give way to the aircraft at the lower level. However, it is prohibited for any aircraft to overtake another aircraft that is at a final stage of an approach to landing.[12]

7.4 Flight over High Seas

Article 12 of the 1944 Chicago Convention is the only article of the Convention that provides for flight over the high seas. It states that when flying over the high seas the rules in force shall be those established under the 1944 Chicago Convention. It further states that each contracting State undertakes to insure the prosecution of all persons violating the applicable regulations.

Before embarking on a discussion of the substance of the aforementioned article, it is important to note that, as earlier discussed, the same article indicates that each contracting State undertakes to adopt measures to insure that every aircraft flying over or maneuvering over its territory shall comply with its rules and regulations.

The spirit of Article 12 is that each contracting State shall endeavor to keep its own rules and regulations in uniformity with the rules established by the 1944 Chicago Convention and its Annexes, to the greatest possible extent. However, it remains a rule that the rules and regulations of the territory being overflown will always be of primary consideration, particularly in case of a conflict between the two regimes.

Thus, it is important to understand the limit of the territory of the coastal State within the spirit of the law of the sea, to determine the applicable law at a given point when overflying the sea.

Article 2 of the United Nations Convention on the Law of the Sea (UNCLOS) provides the following:

1. The sovereignty of a coastal State extends, beyond its land territory and internal waters, and in the case of an archipelagic State, its archipelagic waters, to an adjacent belt of sea, described as the territorial sea.
2. This sovereignty extends to the air space over the territorial sea as well as to its bed and subsoil.
3. The sovereignty over the territorial sea is exercised subject to this Convention and other rules of international law.

The Convention on the Law of the Sea indicates that the sovereignty of the coastal State ends with the limit of the territorial sea. The 1944 Chicago Convention never intended to depart from the same spirit, as it considers that the air space above the territorial sea is governed primarily by the rules and regulations of the coastal State, although such primacy is not extended to the Exclusive Economic Zone.

Indeed, whereas the territorial sea extends up to 12 Nautical Miles,[13] the Exclusive Economic Zone extends up to 200 Nautical Miles.[14] It goes without saying that even in the event of the existence of a continental shelf extended beyond the Exclusive Economic Zone, as stipulated by Article 78(1) of the UNCLOS, the rights of the coastal State over the continental shelf do not affect the legal status of the superjacent waters or of the air space above those waters.

Article 76(1) of the UNCLOS defines the continental shelf as follows:

> The continental shelf of a coastal State comprises the seabed and subsoil of the submarine areas that extend beyond its territorial sea throughout the natural prolongation of its land territory to the outer edge of the continental margin, or to a distance of 200 nautical miles from the baselines from which the breadth of the territorial sea is measured where the outer edge of the continental margin does not extend up to that distance.

Indeed, the exercise of the right of coastal States over the continental shelf is limited to exploring it and exploiting its natural resources[15] and cannot be extended to the airspace.

The aforementioned Article 12 provides that the rules adopted under the 1944 Chicago Convention shall apply in the high seas. The difficulty raised by this phraseology is that no further laws applying exclusively to the High Seas were adopted.

This has left Article 12 to be subjected to various interpretations, including the understanding that, wherever applicable, Annex 2 (providing for the rules of the air) shall be considered the applicable regulation.[16]

7.5 Nonscheduled Flight

The 1944 Chicago Convention does not define the concept of nonscheduled flight as it does not define the concept of scheduled flight. However, the ICAO Council adopted the definition of scheduled international air service from which a nonscheduled flight can be understood.

Accordingly, a scheduled international air service should cumulatively meet the following requirements:

(a) It passes through the air space over the territory of more than one state.

(b) It is performed by aircraft for the transport of passengers, mail, or cargo for remuneration, in such a manner that each flight is open to use by members of the public.

(c) It is operated to serve traffic between the same two or more points, either

    (i) according to a published timetable or

    (ii) with flights so regular or frequent that they constitute a recognizable systematic series.[17]

Thus, any commercial flight other than a scheduled flight is considered a nonscheduled flight. It goes without saying that, in its beginning, the civil aviation industry was understood mainly to cater to scheduled international flights, which then constituted a large percentage of all commercial flights, leaving a minor portion to nonscheduled flights.

With the phenomenon of charter flights gaining more ground progressively, nonscheduled flights have become more frequent, making it necessary for this topic to be efficiently addressed.

Indeed, in its first paragraph, Article 5 of the 1944 Chicago Convention provides the following:

> Each contracting State agrees that all aircraft of the other contracting States, being aircraft not engaged in scheduled international air services shall have the right, subject to the observance of the terms of this Convention, to make flights into or in transit nonstop across its territory and to make stops for non-traffic purposes without the necessity of obtaining prior permission, and subject to the right of the State flown over to require landing.

The next paragraph stipulates the following:

> Each contracting State nevertheless reserves the right, for reasons of safety of flight, to require aircraft desiring to proceed over regions that are inaccessible or without adequate air navigation facilities to follow prescribed routes, or to obtain special permission for such flights.

Hence, the law requires that such air carriage of passengers, cargo, or mail is performed for remuneration; private jets and humanitarian flights are considered not governed by this legislation. Furthermore, the Convention clearly indicates that nonscheduled flights are also subject to the provisions of Article 7, according to which States parties have the right to refuse permission to the aircraft of other contracting States to take on in its territory passengers, mail, and cargo carried for remuneration or hire and destined for another point within its territory.

In general terms, scheduled flights are flights that are performed for remuneration according to a published timetable or that are regular and frequent as to constitute a recognizably systematic series. Such flights are open to direct booking by members of the public. The Convention has established that it shall be the right of the Contracting State to establish laws and regulations or conditions as it deems fit to regulate them. Thus, nonscheduled flights are to be understood as any other flight operated for remunerative purposes that is not necessarily part of a published timetable.

CHAPTER 8

The Warsaw System of Liability

8.1 From 1929 to 1999

Until 1929 the question of liability of the carrier and the question of rights of individuals in case of breach or any other dispute arising from the execution of an international air carriage contract had not been addressed. Air law had been concerned with regulating the relationship between airlines and States, thus leaving the relationship between airlines and their clients in limbo.

This lacuna left the contract of carriage by air to be regulated by domestic laws as it would soon create the difficult question of conflict of laws, among others, including a possibility that different judges would award compensations that would vary depending on their jurisdiction.

Accordingly, the 1929 Warsaw Convention was alleged to provide a set of rules that would address uniformly the question of liability of the carrier as it was then called the 1929 Warsaw Convention for the Unification of Certain Rules Relating to International Carriage by Air.

In reality, at that time, when the industry was still in its infancy, there were concerns that the industry needed to be protected against certain claims for compensation that might ruin certain airlines if the law did not protect them by limiting their liabilities in case of accidents and other related damages.

However, following various dissatisfactions, the 1929 Warsaw Convention was subject to some modification and amendments and supplemented by various instruments, including the following:

- The Protocol to Amend the Convention for the Unification of Certain Rules Relating to International Carriage by Air signed at Warsaw on October 12, 1929
- The Convention, Supplementary to the Warsaw Convention, for the Unification of Certain Rules Relating to International Carriage by Air Performed by a Person Other than the Contracting Carrier, signed at Guadalajara on September 18, 1961
- The Protocol to Amend the Convention for the Unification of Certain Rules Relating to International Carriage by Air signed at Warsaw on October 12, 1929 as Amended by the Protocol Done at The Hague on September 28, 1955 and signed at Guatemala City on March 8, 1971
- The Additional Protocols Nos. 1 to 3 and Montreal Protocol No. 4 to amend the Warsaw Convention as amended by The Hague Protocol or the Warsaw Convention as amended by both The Hague Protocol and the Guatemala City Protocol signed at Montreal on September 25, 1975
- The Convention for the Unification of certain rules for international carriage by air signed in Montreal on May 28, 1999[1]

Thus, Article 1(2) of the 1929 Warsaw Convention defines the concept of international carriage to mean any carriage in which the place of departure and the place of destination are situated either within the territories of two States parties or the territory of a single State party if there is an agreed place to stop within the territory of another State, even if that State is not a State party. This definition excludes carriage between two points within the territory of a single State party without an agreed stopping place within the territory of another State, commonly referred to as domestic flights.

According to Article 3, a document of carriage is issued to the passenger and shall constitute the contract between the passenger and the carrier. It shall indicate the place of departure and the place of destination. As indicated earlier, if the place of departure and the place of destination are within the territory of one State and there is one or more agreed stopping place(s) within the territory of another State, an indication to that effect should appear on the issued document to establish the international character of the flight.

Indeed, Article 3 (4) provides the following:

> The passenger shall be given written notice to the effect that where this Convention is applicable it governs and may limit the liability of carriers in respect of death or injury and for destruction or loss of, or damage to, baggage, and for delay.

It is upon the carrier to make sure that no passenger is embarked without the required documentation, including their ticket, as lack of such documentation does not nullify the existence of the contract between the parties, which shall, in any event, produce its legal effects.

Furthermore, if the said documentation does not have a clear mention of the applicability of the limitation of liability, such limitation cannot be assumed unless indicated on such documentation that stands for the contract between the carrier and the passengers. It is equally important to note that such limits do not apply if it is proven that the damage was a result of the misconduct of the carrier.

In case of a cargo carriage, an air waybill shall be delivered or any other means that preserves the record of the carriage to be performed may be substituted for the delivery of an air waybill.[2] The loss or damage of such document of the passenger or their luggage and cargo does not result in the loss of rights pertaining to such documents, which can always be proved by other means, including indications of Article 11.[3]

8.2 The Court's Jurisdiction

As far as the court's jurisdiction is concerned, the Warsaw System provides for four possibilities. Thus, the plaintiff may initiate their court action before the court of the domicile of the carrier or of its principal place of business or where it has a place of business through which the contract has been made or before the court at the place of destination.

A fifth possibility is provided for by Article 33(2), which is the passenger's principal and permanent place of residence; however, such possibility is limited to claims related to death and injury of the passenger and not applicable to other claims, namely, damages related to the carriage of goods and luggage.

8.3 Liability of the Carrier

The Warsaw System limits the liability of the carrier to damage sustained in case of death or bodily injury.[4] The Convention does not define the concept of bodily harm nor does it provide for psychological harm. It rather creates a condition that the accident that caused the death or injury should have taken place on board the aircraft or in the course of any of the operations of embarking or disembarking. As stated by J. Brent Alldredge, the concept of bodily injury, as used in Article 17, has given rise to much litigation, disputing not only its meaning but also its scope of application.[5]

Whereas the English version provides that:

> The carrier is liable for damage sustained in the event of the death or wounding of a passenger or any other bodily injury suffered by a passenger, if the accident which caused the damage so sustained took place on board the aircraft or in the course of any of the operations of embarking or disembarking.

Interestingly, the French text of Article 17 stipulates the following:

> *Le transporteur est responsable du dommage survenu en cas de mort, de blessure ou de toute autre lésion corporelle subie par un voyageur lorsque l'accident qui a causé le dommage s'est produit à bord de l'aéronef ou au cours de toutes opérations d'embarquement et de débarquement.*

If the phrase *blessure ou toute autre lésion corporelle* is translated to mean injury or any other bodily harm, the Convention would hardly be interpreted to exclude psychological harm, which obviously could be considered harm other than an injury. However, most of the common law courts have failed to reach that conclusion.[6]

The Convention further establishes the liability of the carrier for damage sustained in case of destruction or loss of, or of damage to, baggage, though on the condition that the event that caused the destruction, loss, or damage took place on board the aircraft or during any period within which the checked baggage was in the charge of the carrier.[7]

It is noticeable that the liability of the carrier is extended to checked and unchecked baggage, commonly called hand language, usually carried by the passengers in the cabin.

The Convention creates liability for damage caused by a delay of passengers, baggage, or cargo, except when the carrier took all required measures to avoid the damage or if such measures were impossible to be taken.

The Convention has implicitly created a period of twenty-one days that could be considered as a grace period for any delayed luggage, after which period any luggage that will not have been received by the passenger will be considered lost and the owner shall be entitled to compensation.[8]

In case of a cargo carrier, the liability of the carrier is established when there has been destruction or loss of, or damage to, cargo, again on the condition that the event that caused the damage so sustained took place during the carriage by air.[9]

However, there are exceptions to such liability if the destruction, loss of, or damage to, the cargo resulted from the defect or vice of the cargo, or if such damage resulted from the defective packaging of the cargo, provided the packaging was not done by the staff of the carrier or their agent.

It should be noted that the liability of the carrier cannot be engaged in any case where the damage is a result of an armed conflict or if such damage is a result of a decision of a public authority, for instance, where the public authority denies exit, transit, or entry of the cargo.[10] However, if the airline did not meet the requirements for exit, transit, or entry of cargo, they cannot be exonerated of their responsibility under the aforementioned legal provision, which applies only if the denial is a result of the abuse of powers by the public authority.

It should be indicated that if the carrier proves that the damage was caused or contributed to by the negligence or other wrongful act or omission of the person claiming compensation, or the person from whom he or she derives his or her rights, the carrier shall be wholly or partly exonerated from its liability to the claimant to the extent that such negligence or wrongful act or omission caused or contributed to the damage.[11]

The same would apply when, because of the death or injury of a passenger, compensation is claimed by a person other than the passenger. The carrier shall likewise be wholly or partly exonerated from its liability to the extent that it proves that the damage was caused or contributed to by the negligence or other wrongful act or omission of that passenger.[12]

8.4 Compensation for Damage

The compensation for damage has been one of the thorniest aspects of the entire Warsaw System. Article 22(1) of the 1929 Warsaw Convention limited the compensation in case of injury or death of a passenger to 125,000 Gold Francs, approximately US$8,300.[13] However, it is Article 22(1) of the 1955 Hague Protocol that amended the earlier article and provided that, in the carriage of persons, the liability of the carrier for each passenger is limited to the sum of 250,000 Gold Francs, thus doubling the Warsaw Convention's limit to approximately US$16,600 in cases of personal injury or death.

Interestingly, certain airlines which were not satisfied by the Warsaw System initiated the 1995 Intercarrier Agreement on Passenger Liability with the aim to

> waive the limitation of liability on recoverable compensatory damages in article 22 paragraph 1 of the Warsaw Convention as to claims for death, wounding or other bodily injuries of a passenger within the meaning of article 17 of the Convention, so that recoverable compensatory damages may be determined and awarded by reference to the law of the domicile of the passenger.[14]

Mainly, the Agreement is understood to have brought a twofold innovation: in international air travel, there shall be no liability limitation on compensatory damages, and the compensatory damages will be awarded according to the law of the passenger's domicile,[15] famously considered the fifth jurisdiction.

It further provides that the signatories reserve all available defenses pursuant to the provisions of the Convention, though stating that "any carrier may waive any defense, including the waiver of any defense up to a specified monetary amount of recoverable compensatory damages, as circumstances may warrant."[16]

Considering that the 1995 Intercarrier Agreement was signed by airlines, it remains an understanding between private entities, namely, airlines and their passengers and could not become a treaty; subsequently, it could by no means amend the Warsaw System, which is an agreement between States. However, the 1995 Intercarrier Agreement remains binding between the parties concerned and enforceable by competent courts.

It is with respect to the implementation of the main agreement that a series of implementing agreements were signed as part of the follow-up process to the 1995 Agreement, including the 1996 IATA Intercarrier, implementing the Agreement. Later, the US Department of Transport approved the IATA Agreements in January 1997, and the European Commission approved them in February 1997, thus making them applicable within their respective jurisdictions.

Considering the gap that had widened between the Intercarrier Agreement and the Warsaw System, States negotiated the 1999 Montreal Convention for the Unification of Certain Rules for International Carriage by Air, which substantially made changes to the Warsaw System by providing in Article 21, on Compensation in Case of Death or Injury of Passengers, "damages arising under paragraph 1 of article 17 not exceeding 100 000 Special Drawing

Rights for each passenger, the carrier shall not be able to exclude or limit its liability."

Its paragraph 2 provides the following:

> The carrier shall not be liable for damages arising under paragraph 1 of Article 17 to the extent that they exceed for each passenger 100,000 Special Drawing Rights if the carrier proves that
> (a) such damage was not due to the negligence or other wrongful act or omission of the carrier or its servants or agents or
> (b) such damage was solely due to the negligence or other wrongful act or omission of a third party.

Three scenarios could be envisaged by the application of the Article. The first is the strict liability of the carrier, that is, in case of an accident that has resulted in the death or injury of a passenger, the claimant is ipso facto entitled to compensation up to 100,000 SDRs without having to prove any fault or negligence of the carrier.

However, if the claimant could prove that the accident was caused by the negligence or other wrongful act or omission of the carrier, its servants, or its agents they could claim an unlimited amount of compensation. Obviously, such an amount is most likely to go beyond the 100,000 SDRs ceiling.

Conversely, if the carrier proves that the accident did not result from the negligence or other wrongful act or omission of the carrier, its servants, or its agents or proves that such negligence, fault, or omission resulted from a third party, they cannot be liable for any compensation amount exceeding 100,000 SDRs. However, such proof does not exonerate the carrier from the 100,000 SDRs liability.

Thus, as stated by Mendes De Leon, the limit on liability in Article 22(1) Warsaw Convention has been removed from the

Montreal Convention, which accordingly sets out a system of un-limited liability for passenger injury claims, though the carrier is also presumed to be liable for the second tier of damages exceeding SDR 100,000.[17]

The same was expressed by Regulation EC No 889/2002 of the European Parliament and of the Council of 13 May 2002 amending Council Regulation (EC) No 2027/97 on air carrier liability in the event of accidents. The 2002 Amendment was indeed adopted to align with the 1997 agreement and the 1999 Chicago Convention as in its Article 7 states the following:

> There are no financial limits to the liability for passenger injury or death. For damages up to 100 000 SDRs ... the air carrier cannot contest compensation claims. Above that amount, the air carrier can defend itself against a claim by proving that it was not negligent or otherwise at fault.[18]

Thus, as stated by Lisa Tomas, the Warsaw Convention, which has been largely replaced by the Montreal Convention of 1999, gave a legal basis to unlimited passenger liability and created a two-tier system of compensation in case of death or injury.[19]

According to the two-tier system, the compensation in case of death or injury of a passenger for damages arising under paragraph 1 of Article 17 not exceeding 100,000 SDR is strictly payable by the air carriers. If the claimant proves that the damages caused are due to the negligence, other wrongful act, or omission of the carrier, its servants, or its agents, then the air carrier becomes liable to make full compensation without any limitation.[20]

When the damage to the baggage or cargo is occasioned by delay in the carriage of the same, such damage engages the liability of the carrier unless the carrier proves that they took all measures to prevent such damage or that such measures were not possible to be taken.[21] Thus, a limited compensation of 4,150 SDRs shall be given to each passenger in case of damage caused by such delay.[22]

In case of destruction, loss, damage, or delay of baggage, the compensation is limited to 1,000 SDRs for each passenger unless the passenger has made a special declaration of interest in delivery at the destination and has paid a supplementary sum if the case so requires.[23]

In case of the carriage of cargo, the liability of the carrier in the case of destruction, loss, damage, or delay is limited to a sum of 17 SDRs per kilogram, unless the consignor has made a special declaration of interest in delivery at the destination and has paid a supplementary sum if the case so requires. [24]

CHAPTER 9

The International Civil Aviation Organization (ICAO)

ICAO was created pursuant to Article 43 of the 1944 Chicago Convention, which stated, "An organization to be named the International Civil Aviation Organization is formed by the Convention ..." It shall be recalled that the ICAO came in replacement of the Provisional International Civil Aviation Organization (PICAO), which had been established by section 1 of the Agreement on International Civil Aviation.[1]

PICAO was designed to last for an interim period, until the 1944 Chicago Convention entered into force and its subsequent creation of the ICAO or until another conference on civil aviation was to decide on its fate; however, the Agreement stipulated that the interim period was not to last for more than three years in any event. Fortunately, before the interim three-year period elapsed, the Convention had entered into force, and there was no need to renew the PICAO mandate as it was replaced by ICAO.[2]

9.1 Objectives

According to Article 44 of the 1944 Chicago Convention:

> The aims and objectives of the Organization are to develop
> the principles and techniques of international air navigation

and to foster the planning and development of international
air transport to

(a) insure the safe and orderly growth of international civil
aviation throughout the world;

(b) encourage the arts of aircraft design and operation for
peaceful purposes;

(c) encourage the development of airways, airports, and air
navigation facilities for international civil aviation;

(d) meet the needs of the peoples of the world for safe, regular,
efficient, and economical air transport;

(e) prevent economic waste caused by unreasonable competition;

(f) insure that the rights of contracting States are fully respected
and that every contracting State has a fair opportunity to
operate international airlines;

(g) avoid discrimination between contracting States;

(h) promote safety of flight in international air navigation; and

(i) promote generally the development of all aspects of international civil aeronautics.

However, as indicated by Mendes De Lion, economic regulations in international air transport services are rather left to be
addressed by bilateral air services agreements between States or
other arrangements and are as such not addressed by ICAO.[3]

9.2 Permanent Seat and Regional Offices

Whereas section 2 of the Interim Agreement had already provided that the seat of the Organization shall be located in Canada,
Article 45 of the 1944 Chicago Convention provides that the permanent seat of the Organization shall be at such a place as shall
be determined at the final meeting of the Interim Assembly of
PICAO set up by the Interim Agreement on International Civil

Aviation signed at Chicago on December 7, 1944. Thus, its permanent seat is located in Montreal, Canada.

To better serve contracting States and to maintain liaison with non-States parties, the Organization has established regional offices in various parts of the world. In Asia, the regional office is located in Bangkok; for the Middle East, ICAO's regional office is in Cairo; for Western and Central Africa, the office is located in Dakar; for North and Central America and the Caribbean, the regional office is in Mexico; for Eastern and Southern Africa, the regional office is located in Nairobi; and for Europe and the North Atlantic, the regional office is located in Paris.[4]

9.3 Membership

Article 92(a) stipulates that adherence to the Convention and subsequent membership to the Organization is open to members of the United Nations and States associated with them and to States that remained neutral during the "present world conflict."

This reflects how the political context at the time of the drafting of the Convention influenced the outcome of the final text. For instance, in its sixty-fifth plenary meeting of December 14, 1946, the UNGA approved, among others, the agreement of special agencies, although it approved the ICAO Agreement on condition that the Organization complies with any decision of the UNGA regarding Franco Spain.[5] Such a decision might rather be motivated by political considerations.

It is in compliance with such requirement that ICAO adopted Article 93 bis, which provides the following:

a) Notwithstanding the provisions of Articles 91, 92, and 93,
   1. A State whose government the General Assembly of the United Nations has recommended be debarred from membership in international agencies established by

> > or brought into relationship with the United Nations shall automatically cease to be a member of the International Civil Aviation Organization.
> >
> > 2. A State that has been expelled from membership in the United Nations shall automatically cease to be a member of the International Civil Aviation Organization unless the General Assembly of the United Nations attaches to its act of expulsion a recommendation to the contrary.
>
> b) A State that ceases to be a member of the International Civil Aviation Organization as a result of the provisions of paragraph (a) above may, after approval by the General Assembly of the United Nations, be readmitted to the International Civil Aviation Organization upon application and approval by a majority of the Council.
>
> c) Members of the Organization who are suspended from the exercise of the rights and privileges of membership in the United Nations shall, upon the request of the latter, be suspended from the rights and privileges of membership in this Organization.

The admission of a new member State is, thus, governed by Article 93, according to which such admission is subject to a positive vote of four-fifths of member States, meaning 156 States with the current member States' number. The condition that, in each case, the assent of any State invaded or attacked during the war by the State seeking admission shall be necessary has been abandoned. Indeed, as a specialized agency of the UN, membership of ICAO is open for States that are members of the UN.

9.4 Organs

Chapters 8 to 10 of the 1944 Chicago Convention provide for the organs of ICAO.

9.4.1 The Assembly

Article 48 provides for the Assembly, which is the principal organ of the Organization. Accordingly, although Article 48(a) had initially provided that ordinary sessions of the Assembly were to be scheduled annually, this provision was later amended. Currently, the Assembly meets at least once every three years.[6]

As far as the Assembly's extraordinary sessions are concerned, the Convention and the Rules provide for the possibility of holding such sessions whenever there is a pressing agenda that requires the decision of an extraordinary session of the Assembly. Initially, the same Article 48(a) had provided that such sessions can be held at any time, upon either the call of the Council or the request of any ten contracting States; however, in its fourteenth session of 1962, the text was amended as it now provides that the extraordinary session of the Assembly may be held at any time upon the call of the Council or at the request of not less than one-fifth of the total number of contracting States.[7] The current member States being 193, one-fifth of the same will make it 39 States, instead of 10, as previously provided for.

The plenary sessions of the Assembly are constituted by representatives of every member State. Its decisions are taken by votes, for which every State is equally entitled to one vote. According to Rule 43, each contracting State represented by an accredited delegation shall be entitled to one vote unless the voting power of such State has been suspended by the Assembly under the terms of the Convention.[8]

There is a requirement that the quorum should be obtained, for the validity of the plenary meeting. Accordingly, Rule 28 provides that a majority of the contracting States shall constitute a quorum for the plenary meetings of the Assembly.[9] With the current number of States parties, it takes at least ninety-seven States to have the quorum for the meeting.

Once the Assembly is duly convened, Article 49 provides for the powers and duties of the Assembly:

(a) Elect at each meeting its President and other officers.

(b) Elect the contracting States to be represented on the Council, following the provisions of Chapter IX.

(c) Examine and take appropriate action on the reports of the Council and decide on any matter referred to it by the Council.

(d) Determine its own rules of procedure and establish such subsidiary commissions as it may consider to be necessary or desirable.

(e) Vote an annual budget and determine the financial arrangements of the Organization, in accordance with the provisions of Chapter XII.

(f) Review expenditures and approve the accounts of the Organization.

(g) Refer, at its discretion, to the Council, to subsidiary commissions, or to any other body any matter within its sphere of action.

(h) Delegate to the Council the powers and authority necessary or desirable for the discharge of the duties of the Organization and revoke or modify the delegations of authority at any time.

(i) Carry out the appropriate provisions of Chapter XIII.

(j) Consider proposals for the modification or amendment of the provisions of this Convention and, if it approves of the proposals, recommend them to the contracting States in accordance with the provisions of Chapter XXI.

(k) Deal with any matter within the sphere of action of the Organization not specifically assigned to the Council.

9.4.2 The Council

Initially, Article 50(a) of the 1944 Chicago Convention provided that the Council shall be composed of twenty-one contracting States elected by the Assembly. Following the constant growth of the number of member States, the Article has undergone four amendments, the fourth amendment having been done during the twenty-eighth Session (Extraordinary) held on 25 October 1990 in Montreal that raised the number of Council members from thirty-three to thirty-six.

A fifth amendment of 1 October 2016 that suggested the number of Council members to be raised to forty has not yet entered into force.[10] The Protocol shall come into force on the date of deposit of the 128th instrument of ratification. Till date the Protocol is yet to reach 100 ratifications.

The Convention provides that an election shall be held at the first meeting of the Assembly and thereafter every three years. Elected members of the Council shall hold office until the next election. The Rules provide that each contracting State that intends to stand for election to the Council may at any time inform the Secretary-General, who shall publish a list showing the names of all the States that have notified him of their intention.

Rule 55 (a) provides the following:

The election of the Council shall be so conducted as to enable adequate representation on the Council to be given to the contracting States described in Article 50 (b) of the Convention and shall be held in three parts as follows:

i.   The first part—election of States of chief importance in air transport—shall be held within four days of the opening of the session.

ii. The second part—election of States not already elected in the first part but which make the largest contribution to the

provision of facilities for international civil air navigation—
shall be held immediately after the first part of the election.

iii   The third part—election of States not elected in either the
first or the second part, whether or not they were candidates
in either of those parts and whose designation will ensure that
all the major geographical areas of the world are represented
on the Council—shall be held as soon as possible after the
expiry of twenty-four hours following the publication of
the list of candidates mentioned in Rule 58 (b).

9.4.3 The Air Navigation Commission (ANC)

The ANC is the most technical body of ICAO. Its mandate is described in Article 57 of the 1944 Chicago Convention as follows:

(a) Consider, and recommend to the Council for adoption,
modifications of the Annexes to this Convention.
(b) Establish technical subcommissions on which any contracting State may be represented, if it so desires.
(c) Advise the Council concerning the collection and communication to the contracting States of all information
that it considers necessary and useful for the advancement
of air navigation.

Although the ANC's task is described by the Convention it is important to note that Article 56 stipulates that:

> The Air Navigation Commission shall be composed of twelve
> members appointed by the Council from among persons nom-
> inated by contracting States [...] The Council shall request all
> contracting States to submit nominations. The President of the
> Air Navigation Commission shall be appointed by the Council.

Having been appointed by the Council does not undermine the independence of the ANC from the Council, which it still serves as an advisory body.[11] Indeed, considering the technical aspect of issues at hand, the ANC itself works through different panels. It should be mentioned that ANC members are highly qualified and experts in the science and practice of aeronautics.[12]

Thus, ICAO delegates its authority to the panel through the ANC. It is the ANC that establishes its panels, determines its members, their working program, and their terms of reference, as well as the time frame given to them for a particular assignment. Once a panel is assigned a task, it works independently.

Currently, the ANC works through the following panels: Aerodrome Design and Operations Panel, Accident Investigation Panel, Airworthiness Panel, Air Traffic Management Operations Panel, Air Traffic Management Requirements and Performance Panel, Communications Panel, Dangerous Goods Panel, Flight Operations Panel, Frequency Spectrum Management Panel, Instrument Flight Procedures Panel, Information Management Panel, Meteorology Panel, Navigation Systems Panel, Remotely Piloted Aircraft Systems Panel, Separation and Airspace Safety Panel, Safety Management Panel, and Surveillance Panel.

The importance of the panels to the aviation industry cannot be overrated. If the development and update of the international standards and recommended practices and procedures for air navigation are considered the main mission of ICAO itself, it goes without saying how vital the work of the panel is to this industry, because it is from there that such regulations emanate.[13]

9.4.4 The Secretariat

There is blunt silence in the Convention as far as the Secretariat of the Organization is concerned. Indeed, the Convention does not even mention the word Secretariat. Article 58 is the only relevant provision that stipulates that the Council shall determine the method of appointment and termination of appointment, the training, and the salaries, allowances, and conditions of service of the Secretary-General and other personnel of the Organization.

It can be deduced from the aforementioned provision that once the Secretary-General has been appointed, they can only operate from a Secretariat. Indeed, the Secretariat consists of five bureaus: the Air Navigation Bureau, the Air Transport Bureau, the Technical Co-operation Bureau, the Legal Affairs and External Relations Bureau, and the Bureau of Administration and Services.

9.5 Duties

The duties performed by ICAO make it an exceptional institution within the entire UN framework. It will be an exaggeration to see the work of ICAO as a legislative, judicial, and implementing mandate. However, a close look at its works shows some indications in this respect.

9.5.1 Quasi-Legislative Duties

The adoption of SARPs and their incorporation into the Annexes to the Chicago Convention constitute one of the key functions of the Council.

Article 37 of the 1944 Chicago Convention states the following:

> Each contracting State undertakes to collaborate in securing the highest practicable degree of uniformity in regulations, standards, procedures, and organization concerning aircraft, personnel,

airways, and auxiliary services in all matters in which such uniformity will facilitate and improve air navigation.

To this end, the International Civil Aviation Organization shall
adopt and amend from time to time, as may be necessary, international standards and recommended practices and procedures
dealing with

(a) communications systems and air navigation aids, including
    ground marking;
(b) characteristics of airports and landing areas;
(c) rules of the air and air traffic control practices;
(d) licensing of operating and mechanical personnel;
(e) airworthiness of aircraft;
(f) registration and identification of aircraft;
(g) collection and exchange of meteorological information;
(h) log books;
(i) aeronautical maps and charts;
(j) customs and immigration procedures; and
(k) aircraft in distress and investigation of accidents, and such other
    matters concerned with the safety, regularity, and efficiency of
    air navigation as may from time to time appear appropriate.

The legal basis of the mandate given to the Council to adopt the
standards and recommended practices is, therefore, clearly established; however, there is still a need to discuss the legal nature of
such standards and practices.

One would take note of the fact that the aforementioned Article
indicates that States parties undertake to collaborate in securing
the highest practicable degree of uniformity. Such formulation
would be hardly used for any binding text expected to be part of
international law. Indeed, this could be viewed as simply an act
of commitment of States to endeavor to the best of their ability to
secure the highest standard they can, but not the highest standard
that such States must achieve.

Further, Article 38 providing for departure from international standards and practices is indicative. Article 38 stipulates the following:

> Any State that finds it impracticable to comply in all respects with any such international standards or procedure, or to bring its regulations or practices into full accord with any international standard or procedure after the amendment of the latter, or that deems it necessary to adopt regulations or practices differing in any particular respect from those established by an international standard, shall give immediate notification to the International Civil Aviation Organization of the differences between its practice and that established by the international standard...

Accordingly, the only conventional obligation binding upon States parties is to notify the Council of the differences between the State practice concerned and the international standards. The consequence of such notification would be that the given State would not be expected to comply beyond what is practical to it. This would seem to indicate that the Convention itself does not consider the standards and practices as binding.

Nevertheless, it is important to highlight that the notification of such differences serves an additional purpose to inform the rest of the world aviation community of such differences to avoid incidents that might be a result of the application of the standards where they might not be applicable. This justifies the obligation created upon the Council to notify all other States of the difference that exists between one or more features of an international standard and the corresponding national practice of that State.[14]

Thus, a State that did not notify the Council of any difference with its practices is expected to apply the international standards, however, to give the standards a legal force, a State must domesticate them by an act of the parliament that needs to be adopted according to the constitutional laws of the given State to transpose the standards and practices into domestic laws.

As far as the adoption of the standards and practices is concerned, such adoption is subjected to a vote of two-thirds of the Council. Once the standards have been adopted, the Council must circulate them to all States members. The standards shall then become effective, three months after their submission to States parties if the majority of contracting States do not register their disapproval of the standards.[15] Therefore, no annex will become applicable unless it has passed the double-layer process, as they are never required to be ratified by States.

It should be indicated that even if the standards and practices are not considered binding, they remain part of the regulatory framework within the aviation industry, albeit as soft law, as their weight cannot be underestimated.

9.5.2 Quasi-Judicial Duties

Article 84 of the 1944 Chicago Convention states the following:

> If any disagreement between two or more contracting States relating to the interpretation or application of this Convention and its Annexes cannot be settled by negotiation, it shall, on the application of any State concerned in the disagreement, be decided by the Council.[16]

Thus far, seven cases have been submitted to the ICAO dispute settlement mechanism.[17] However, the Council has issued its final decision only in two cases. In the two cases, one of the parties appealed to the ICJ. Indeed, the Convention indicates that appeals against the decision of the Council can be submitted to either an ad hoc arbitral tribunal agreed upon between the parties to the dispute or the ICJ.

In four cases, the parties to the conflict decided to settle the dispute through negotiations; in one case, the parties postponed the case indefinitely. These statistics have led some authors to question the efficiency of the Council's dispute settlement mechanism.[18]

A review of the two decided cases will guide the understanding of the mechanism. Indeed, the first case that was decided on by the Council was Pakistan *v.* India in 1971, while the second case was Qatar *v.* Bahrain, Egypt, United Arab Emirates, and Saudi Arabia.

9.5.2.1 Pakistan v. India Case

India and Pakistan were parties to a Bilateral Transit Agreement that conferred similar privileges in respect of scheduled international air services to overfly or make non-traffic stops in the territories of the other State.[19]

India would submit that, as a result of political turmoil followed by armed conflicts between the two States, the Transit Agreement was suspended and was never reinstated, although as the political tension deescalated, the two States allowed each other's aircrafts to overfly each other's territory under a special agreement of 1966, which never included the right to land in each other's territory.[20]

However, Pakistan submitted that over-flights across each other's territory were resumed based on the Convention and the Transit Agreement, meaning this included not only the right to fly over the other's territory but also the right to land for non-traffic purposes. Further, Pakistan would dispute the existence of any special agreement other than the Transit Agreement.[21]

On 4 February 1971, India withdrew the permission for Pakistan aircraft to overfly India, following an incident involving the diversion of an Indian aircraft to Pakistan. As Pakistan complained to the ICAO Council under Article 84 of the 1944 Chicago Convention and Article II of the International Air Services Transit Agreement.

Whereas Section 1 of Article II of the Transit Agreement provides that "a contracting State which deems that action by another contracting State under this Agreement is causing injustice or hardship to it, may request the Council to examine the situation…," Section 2 of Article II of the Transit Agreement states that the following:

> If any disagreement between two or more contracting States relating to the interpretation or application of this Agreement cannot be settled by negotiation, the provisions of Chapter XVIII of the above-mentioned Convention shall be applicable in the same manner as provided therein concerning any disagreement relating to the interpretation or application of the above-mentioned Convention.

Whereas Pakistan contended that the refusal of India to let Pakistan aircraft overfly India's territory amounted to a disagreement between the two States relating to the application of the Convention and the Transit Agreement, India submitted that such conduct amounted to action under the Transit Agreement.

India would further argue that the Council's jurisdiction is limited to a disagreement related to the interpretation or application of the Convention or the Transit Agreement and does not extend to disputes related to termination or suspension of the Convention or the Transit Agreement. However, the Council rather found that it had jurisdiction to decide on the case.

As India was not satisfied by the ICAO decision of August 30, 1971, it appealed against the decision before the ICJ. In its judgment of August 18, 1972, the ICJ affirmed the existence of a "disagreement" relating to the application of the treaties and that there can, therefore, be no doubt about the character of the case presented by Pakistan to the Council. The Court further found that it was essentially a case of breaches of the treaties, of which in order to make a determination, the Council would inevitably be obliged to interpret and apply such treaties.[22]

Thus, the Court concluded that the Council of ICAO was competent to entertain the application and complaint brought before it by the Government of Pakistan on March 3, 1971 and consequently rejected the appeal made to the Court by the Government of India against the decision of the Council on the alleged lack of jurisdiction.

9.5.2.2 Qatar v. Bahrain, Egypt, United Arab Emirate, and Saudi Arabia

In November 2013, the States of Kuwait, Qatar, and Saudi Arabia signed the Riyadh Agreement, according to which, among other things, no State party should harbor or naturalize any citizen of the Gulf Cooperation Council States, hereinafter "the GCC states" who has an activity that opposes his country's regime, except with the approval of his country, and no support to deviant groups that oppose their States or support for antagonistic media.

The agreement further indicated that no support should be given to the Muslim Brotherhood or any of the organizations or individuals that threaten the security and stability of the Council's members States through direct security work or political influence and that no support should be given to any faction in Yemen that could pose a threat to countries neighboring Yemen.

Interestingly, what is referred to as the Mechanism Implementing the Riyadh Agreement would stipulate that States parties commit themselves to ensure that any media channels owned or supported by any GCC member should not discuss any disrespectful subjects to any GCC State directly 0r indirectly.

Further, the Supplementary Riyadh Agreement of November 16, 2014 provides that members States should not give refuge, employment, or support, whether directly or indirectly, whether domestically or abroad, to any person or a media apparatus that harbors inclinations harmful to any GCC State and that all States should cease all media activity directed against the Arab Republic of Egypt in all media platforms whether directly or indirectly, including all the offenses broadcast on Al-Jazeera.

Following allegations of violation of the aforementioned agreements on 5th June 2017, the Governments of Bahrain, Egypt, Saudi Arabia, and the United Arab Emirates decided to take a series of restrictive measures relating to terrestrial, maritime, and aerial lines of communication with Qatar, which included certain aviation restrictions.

As a result of these restrictions, all Qatar-registered aircraft were barred by the Appellants from landing at or departing from their airports and were denied the right to overfly their respective territories, including the territorial seas within the relevant flight information regions. Certain restrictions also applied to non-Qatar-registered aircraft flying to and from Qatar, which were required to obtain prior approval from the civil aviation authorities of the four States.[23]

Thus, on October 30, 2017, pursuant to Article 84 of the Chicago Convention, Qatar filed an application to the ICAO Council, in which it claimed that the aviation restrictions adopted by Bahrain, Egypt, Saudi Arabia, and the United Arab Emirates violated their obligations under the Chicago Convention.

On March 19, 2018, Bahrain, Egypt, Saudi Arabia, and the United Arab Emirates, as respondents before the ICAO Council, raised two preliminary objections. In the first preliminary objection, they argued that the ICAO Council lacked jurisdiction under the Chicago Convention since the real issue in dispute between the parties involved matters extending beyond the scope of that instrument, including whether the aviation restrictions could be characterized as lawful countermeasures under international law.

In the second preliminary objection, they argued that Qatar had failed to meet the precondition of negotiation outlined in Article 84 of the Chicago Convention, also reflected in Article 2, sub-paragraph *(g)*, of the ICAO Rules for the Settlement of Differences, and, consequently, that the Council lacked jurisdiction to resolve the claims raised by Qatar, or that the application was inadmissible.

However, by a decision dated June 29, 2018, the ICAO Council rejected the two objections. On July 4, 2018, the four States submitted a joint application to the ICJ instituting an appeal against the decision of the Council dated June 29, 2018.

In its judgment of July 14, 2020, the ICJ unanimously rejected the appeal brought by the Kingdom of Bahrain, the Arab Republic of Egypt, the Kingdom of Saudi Arabia, and the United Arab Emirates on July 4, 2018 from the decision of the ICAO Council dated June 29, 2018.

The Court further held that the Council had jurisdiction to entertain the application submitted to it by the Government of the State of Qatar on October 30, 2017 and that the said application is admissible.

Obviously, the two cases that were brought before the ICJ consisted of a contestation of the jurisdiction of the Council and were not to be adjudicated on merit. It has been observed that the Court itself abstained from addressing any matter pertaining to the merit of the cases as that has never been a point of the contest before it.

Contrary to the quasi-legislative role of the Council, which has seen the adoption of nineteen annexes to the 1944 Convention, the adjudicating role of the Council cannot be said to have achieved equal success.

9.5.3 Quasi-Enforcement Duties

Within the UN framework, the ICAO Council is one unique body due to the different roles assigned to it by the 1944 Chicago Convention. Already, the earlier discussed sections would point to an institution that regulates and adjudicates, although a close look at its mandate points to a third assignment.

As discussed, Article 38 creates an obligation for States that find a difference between their practice and the established international standards to notify the Council of such differences. This requirement cannot be compared to the usual reporting mechanism in international law, although it still could be viewed as having been inspired by the same.

Perhaps a more convincing practice would be found in Article 54 (j and k) of the Convention, according to which the Council shall

(j) report to contracting States any infraction of this Convention, as well as any failure to carry out recommendations or determinations of the Council, and

(k) report to the Assembly any infraction of this Convention where a contracting State has failed to take appropriate action within a reasonable time after notice of the infraction.

Although seeing the ICAO Council as an enforcing body could be far-reaching, it remains a fact that the Council performs certain activities that are usually entrusted to enforcement mechanisms.

CHAPTER 10

The International Air Transport Association (IATA)

Founded in Havana, Cuba, on 19 April 1945, the Association has evolved due to many factors, as will be further discussed. Despite being called the International Air Transport Association, the IATA is not an international organization; it is rather a nongovernmental organization incorporated under Canadian domestic law as a non-profit-making association.[1]

The Association was created to represent, lead, and serve airlines in the aviation industry.[2]

10.1 Head Office and Regional Offices

As provided for by Article 3 of the Articles of the Association, hereinafter the Articles, the Association's head office is in Montreal, Canada, but it has five regional offices and over fifty other offices supporting airlines around the world.

The five regional offices are as follows: Madrid for the region of Europe, Amman for Africa and the Middle East region, Singapore for the region of Asia Pacific, Beijing for the region of North Asia, and Miami for the Americas.

10.2 Membership

Article 5(1) of the Articles provides for the following criteria of eligibility:

i.   Operate an Air Service.
ii. Maintain a valid IATA Operational Safety Audit (IOSA) Registration or equivalent as it may be renamed from time to time.
iii. Have operated an Air Service for a period of not less than two years and performed for each of those years at least five million revenue tonne kilometers.

As an association regrouping airlines, it goes without saying that the applicant for its membership must first and foremost be an airline, which is understood as an entity operating air service, which means an airline that offers public transport of passengers and mail cargo by aircraft.[3]

The IATA might have been conceived mainly aiming at bringing together airlines offering international scheduled air services. However, in a short while the reality of air services shifted from that paradigm as nonscheduled flights became part of business. Indeed, as explained by Peter PC Haanappel, chartered only airlines might not have been originally eligible for membership in IATA, nevertheless through an amendment to the Incorporation Act such airlines have been accepted.[4]

Furthermore, even an airline that does not meet the criteria set out in the aforementioned Article 5(1) may still be admitted to membership if the Board considers that to be in the interest of IATA. Such flexibility is not to be considered arbitrary but rather a progressive interpretation of the reality of the air transport industry.

10.3 Fees

IATA depends on the contributions of airlines that are members of the Association. An annual fee is paid by every airline member, and such fee is determined by the Board taking into account various indicators, including the size of the airline concerned.

Indeed, there is a fixed fee payable by all members, although an additional variable fee is calculated for airlines that perform over 5 million international revenue tonne kilometers (RTKMs) per annum.

A tonne-kilometer is generally understood as a metric tonne of revenue load carried per kilometer. Tonne kilometers performed equal the sum of the products obtained by multiplying the total number of tonnes of each category of revenue load carried by the airport-to-airport distance.[5]

10.4 Structure of the Association

The Incorporation Act creates two bodies through which the Association is managed: the General Meeting and the Board of Governors.

10.4.1 The General Meeting

The General Meeting is the highest organ of the Association. According to Article 12(3), it shall exercise all the following powers of the Association:

a. Elect its President
b. Receive nominations from the Nominating Committee and elect members of the Board

c.   Elect the Nominating Committee to make recommenda-
     tions to the next AGM for election to the Board
d.   Establish the rules of the Nominating Committee
e.   Establish IATA Conferences and such groups and sub-
     ordinate bodies as it considers appropriate
f.   Confirm the appointment, term of office, and duties of
     the Director General
g.   Receive and consider reports of the Board, Industry
     Committees, IATA Conferences, and the Director General
h.   Approve the audited annual consolidated financial state-
     ments for the previous year
i.   On the recommendation of the Board, approve the ap-
     plicable Fees and Dues
j.   On the recommendation of the Board, approve the currency
     or currencies in which, and the time by which, such Fees
     and Dues shall be payable
k.   Appoint the external auditor for the current year
l.   Transact any other business as may properly come before
     the AGM

According to the Rules, the annual general meeting (AGM) is usually convened at a place and time agreed to by a previous AGM,
but not more than fifteen months after the previous AGM and not
later than six months after the end of IATA's financial year.

In the absence of such agreement by the previous AGM or
should the Board deem it impractical to hold the AGM at the
place or time so agreed, the Board would decide on the place
and time where the AGM is to be held as it can decide if such a
meeting could be held electronically.[6]

An extraordinary session, named special general meeting
(SGM), may be convened at any time by the Board. However, the
Board should send the notice and the agenda for such a meeting

sixty days before the proposed date of the meeting. The SMG could equally be called for by not less than one-third of the members addressed to the Board. Such a request should indicate a proposed agenda, in which case the meeting should be held not less than sixty days after the request is made.[7]

Although neither the Act nor the Rules provide for substantive grounds that would warrant the request for an SGM, it is generally accepted that whenever there is an urgent matter to be decided by the meeting and that might not wait until the next AGM, the SGM should be called for.

As a matter of rights, all airline members are equally represented at a General Meeting, except when placed under limitation. Whenever a member would fail to pay its dues and interests for a period of more than ninety days, such airline will be placed under limitation and shall consequently lose all rights and privileges of membership during the period that the limitations apply, unless the Board has agreed to alternative financial arrangements.[8]

10.4.2 The Board of Governors

The Board of Governors, hereinafter the Board, is established by the Act of Incorporation. The Board constitutes the Executive Committee of the Association and is accountable to the General Meeting.[9]

According to the Rules and Regulations of the Board of Governors, the Board is mandated to act on behalf of and in the interest of the Association. All members of the Board act as a whole in cooperation and coordination with the Director General.[10]

Further, the Board gives policy directives and guidance to IATA Advisory Councils and their subsidiary bodies. The Board also provides policy guidance to IATA Traffic Conferences and the industry settlement plans, as may be required.[11]

Article 14(8) of the Articles provides for the duties of the Board as follows:

a.   Shall elect the Board Chair

b.   Shall meet immediately before each AGM in the same locality as the AGM (or by electronic means if the AGM is conducted electronically), and hold at least one (1) additional regular meeting each year on a date and at a place fixed by the Board

c.   Shall be vested with executive powers and duties, including the general management and control of the business, affairs, funds, and property of IATA

d.   Shall determine, review, and approve IATA policy within the framework of the Act of Incorporation, these Articles, and the decisions of General Meetings

e.   Shall take action in response to specific requests from Members as it deems appropriate

f.   Shall appoint the Director General, subject to the approval of the AGM, and determine the term of office, duties, and remuneration

g.   Shall appoint the Corporate Secretary, the Chief Financial Officer, and such other officers of IATA as deemed appropriate, who shall be subject to the supervision and authority of the Director General

h.   Shall establish subsidiary corporations, branches, regional, and other offices of IATA anywhere in the world as it considers appropriate

i.   Shall approve the agenda for a General Meeting

j.   Shall approve the Rules and Regulations of the Industry Committees and the Provisions for the Conduct of the IATA Traffic Conferences

k.   Shall establish and determine the membership, duties, and functions of any Committee of the Board

l.   Shall either establish and determine the rules and regulations of any Committee of the Board or authorize any such Committee to adopt its own rules and regulations

m.   Shall recommend to the AGM the fees and dues and the time by which they shall be payable, as well as the currency or currencies in which they are to be paid

n.   Shall consider for approval, applications for membership of IATA

o.   Shall take such action as may be appropriate with respect to the limitation, suspension, or termination of membership

p.   May delegate, as appropriate, authority to Committees of the Board or to the Director General

q.   May adopt and amend its Rules and Regulations as deemed appropriate for the exercise of its executive powers and the performance of its duties

10.4.3 Advisory Councils

According to Article 25(4) of the Articles, the Director General "may, with the approval of the Board, establish one or more Industry Committees to advise on subjects of significant interest to the air transport industry, appoint its members, and dissolve any such Industry Committees at any time."

It is in application of Article 25(4) that the Director General has established Advisory Councils that are considered as Industry Committees. The Advisory Councils are composed of a minimum of twelve and a maximum of twenty experts who are appointed from member airlines and shall serve as representatives of their respective airlines.

Each Advisory Council provides technical advice according to its specific mandate and is expected to accomplish its task within a given time frame. Thus far the Director General has established nine Advisory Councils: the Cargo Advisory Council, the Digital Transformation Advisory Council, the Distribution Advisory Council, the Industry Affairs Advisory Council, the Industry Financial Advisory Council, the Legal Advisory Council, the Operations Advisory Council, the Security Advisory Council, and the Sustainability and Environment Advisory Council.

Individual members of the Advisory Councils shall have the experience and expertise required to make a substantial contribution to the Advisory Council's work. Rule 3(4) stipulates the following:

Appointments shall take into consideration

i.   regional balance;
ii. size of member airline balance;
iii. a combination of continuity and rotation in the Advisory Council membership;
iv. representation of the membership across all of the Advisory Councils;
v.   seniority within the airline of the candidate concerned;
vi. candidates from airlines that share a common ownership structure;
vii. gender diversity; and
viii. the views of the current members of the Advisory Council concerned.[12]

Subject to the approval of the Director General, the Advisory Councils may, in turn, establish Working Groups. Such Working Groups shall provide technical guidance to an Advisory Council and the IATA management on an ongoing basis and work on any other technical matter referred to them by the Director General in consultation with the relevant Advisory Council.

10.4.4 The Traffic Conferences

It is pursuant to Article 33(3)(e) of the Articles, according to which the AGM shall establish IATA Conferences and subordinate bodies as it considers appropriate, that the AGM established the Traffic Conferences. The Provisions for the Conduct of IATA Traffic Conferences gives a list of the various conferences created thus far.

Rule (IV) stipulates the following:

> 5. Subject as hereinafter provided each Passenger Tariff Coordinating Conference shall concern itself with the analysis of relevant operating costs and take action to develop passenger fares and related conditions in respect of the area of authority of such Conference.

> 6. A Composite meeting of Passenger Tariff Conferences shall take action on those matters and practices relating to fare construction and currency rules (other than those which by their terms apply only to one Passenger Tariff Conference), conditions of service, baggage allowance, and charges, remuneration levels of recognized passenger sales intermediaries, and such other matters as may be referred to it by any Passenger Tariff Conference.

> 7. Subject as hereinafter provided each Cargo Tariff Coordinating Conference shall concern itself with the analysis of relevant operating costs and take action to develop cargo rates and related conditions in respect of the area of authority of such Conference.

> 8. A Composite meeting of Cargo Tariff Conferences shall take action on those matters and practices relating to rate construction and currency rules (other than those which by their terms apply only to one Cargo Tariff Conference), remuneration levels of intermediaries engaged in the sale and/or processing of international

air cargo and such other matters as may be referred to it by any
Cargo Tariff Conference.

9. Any action with reference to rates for the carriage of air mail
shall be restricted to recommendations for the carriage of mail
by foreign air carriers.

One of the areas in the aviation industry that has been subject to
a considerable amount of critique and changes is the tariff system. It was first advocated that such pricing should be regulated
and submitted to forces of the market, however the IATA suffers
criticism that the entire process of its deliberations has failed to
include the consumer of the services it manages

It is important to note that considering that at the time of its creation, more airlines were owned by States, a situation which has
been overturned, coupled by the fact that the philosophy of free
market has gained more ground compared with the past decades,
IATA would be obliged to adjust its role accordingly. Thus, many
airlines acknowledge that IATA fares are used to benchmark market forces and as a basis for calculating discount fares.[13]

As more airlines are privatized with fewer tariff coordination
activities and more commercial services, the nature of IATA will
keep changing and will become more of a trade association and
less of a regulatory authority in a liberalized industry.[14]

NOTES

Introduction

1. Future of Aviation available on www.icao.int, last consulted on October 29, 2023.
2. Reza Banakar and Max Travers, Law, Sociology and Method, Theory and Method in Socio-Legal Research, Hart Publishing, 2005, p 8.

Chapter 1: Definition and Historical Development

1. Diederiks-Verschoor, Introduction to Air Law, Wolters Kluwer, 2012, p 1.
2. Michael Milde, International Air Law and ICAO, Eleven International Publishing, 2017, p 1.
3. Bin Cheng, Studies in International Air Law, Brill Nijhoff, 2018, p 35.
4. Jan Wouters, Sten Verhoeven, State Aircraft, Max-Planck Encyclopedia of International Public Law, para 1.
5. It is important to indicate that the current Annex 2 has provisions according to which, except when necessary for take-off or landing or except by permission from the appropriate authority, aircraft shall not be flown over the congested areas of cities, towns, or settlements or an open-air assembly of persons, unless at such a height as will permit, in the event of an emergency arising, a landing to be made without undue hazard to persons or property on the surface. Annex 2 para 3.1.2.
6. Joseph-Michel and Jacques-Étienne Montgolfier, French Aviators, in Britannica Academic, Encyclopædia Britannica, 2013.
7. Elizabeth Bush, Review of The Sheep, the Rooster, and the Duck: A Tale from the Age of Wonder, by Matt Phelan, 75(7) Bull. Cent. Child. Books 227, 2022, p 227.
8. Jean-François Pilâtre de Rozier, in Britannica Academic, Encyclopædia Britannica, 2013.
9. Abbott Lawrence Rotch, Benjamin Franklin and the First Balloons, in American Antiquarian Society, April 1907, pp 259–274.
10. I. H. Ph.Diederiks-Vershoor, An introduction to air law, Wolters Kluwer Law& Business, 9th ed., 2012, p2.
11. Indeed, the first multilateral treaty is the Hague Declaration 1899 on the use of balloons and similar devices as weapons of war. For further details, see The Hague Peace Conference of 1899 and 1907.
12. John Cobb Cooper, The International Air Navigation Conference, 19(2) J. Air L. Com. 127, 1952.
13. For further comment see Louis Rolland, L'accord Franco-Allemand du 26 juillet 1913 relatif à la navigation aérienne, A. Pedone, 1913 and P. P. Haanappel, Bilateral Air Transport Agreements—1913-1980, 5 Md. J. Int'l L. 241, 1980, p 241.
14. Arnold D. McNair, The Beginnings and the Growth of Aeronautical Law, 1 J. Air L. Com. 383, 1930, p 386.
15. See Article 34 of the 1919 Convention Relating to the Regulation of Aerial Navigation.
16. Albert Roper, Recent Developments in International Aeronautical Law, 1 J. Air L. Com. 395, 1930..

17. Michael Milde, International Air Law and ICAO, Eleven International Publishing, 2017, p 10.
18. Paul Stephen Dempsey, Public International Air Law, 2nd ed, 2017, p 20.
19. Alfred Wegerdt, Germany and the Aerial Navigation Convention at Paris, October 13, 1919, 1 J. Air L. Com. 1, 1930, p 2.
20. Stephen Latchford, Habana Convention on Commercial Aviation, 2 J. Air L. Com. 207–210, 1931, p 208.

Chapter 2: The 1944 Chicago Convention and the Freedoms of Air

1. See ICAO, The History of ICAO and the Chicago Convention, https://www.icao.int /about-icao/History/Pages/default.aspx last consulted on June 29, 2023.
2. Bin Cheng, Studies in International Air Law, Brill Nijhoff, 2018, p 85.
3. ECOSOC in its decision relating to the implementation of the Yamoussoukro Declaration concerning the liberalization of access to air transport markets in Africa, ECA/RCID/CM.CIVAC/99/RPT Annex I.
4. See Marc L. J. Dierikx, Shaping World Aviation: Anglo-American Civil Aviation Relations, 1944-1946, 57 J. Air L. Com. 795, 1992.
5. The Annex to the Bermuda agreement stipulates that the designated air carriers of one of the contracting parties shall be accorded in the territory of the other contracting party the use of the said routes at each of the places specified therein of all the airports (being airports designated for international air services), together with ancillary facilities and rights of transit; of stops for non-traffic purposes; and of commercial entry and departure for international traffic in passengers, cargo, and mail in full accord and compliance with the principles recited and agreed in the Final Act of the Conference on Civil Aviation held between the Governments of the United States and of the United Kingdom at Bermuda from January 15 to February 11, 1946.
6. Alan Khee-Jin Tan, Singapore's New Air Services Agreements with the E.U. and the U.K.: Implications for Liberalization in Asia, 73 J. Air L. Com. 351, 2008, p 366.
7. Antigoni Lykotrafiti, Consolidation and Rationalization in the Transatlantic Air Transport Market—Prospects and Challenges for Competition and Consumer Welfare, 76 J. Air L. Com. 661, 2011, p 668.
8. J. P. Hanlon, Sixth Freedom Operations in International Air Transport, 5(3) Tour. Manag. 177–191, 1984.
9. https://ke.usembassy.gov/the-united-states-and-kenya-add-all-cargo-rights-to-air -transport-agreement/.
10. Elmar M. Giemulla, Cabotage, Max-Planck Encyclopedia of International Law.

Chapter 3: Environmental Protection

1. See L. Q. Maurice, D. S. Lee (eds), Assessing Current Scientific Knowledge, Uncertainties and Gaps in Quantifying Climate Change, Noise and Air Quality Aviation Impacts, 2009, see L. Q. Maurice et al., J. Final Report of the International Civil Aviation Organization (ICAO) Committee on Aviation and Environmental Protection (CAEP) Workshop, US Federal Aviation Administration and Manchester Metropolitan University, Washington DC and Manchester, p 17.
2. Dr. med Prince Mbuzukongira suggests that: "Des coup de balles, un pneu qui éclate, un avion qui passe peut causer la production des catécholamines à savoir l'adrénaline et la noradrénaline au niveau de la glande surrénale ce qui a comme effects palpitation, tremblement des extremites, augmentation de tension artérielle, augmentation des péristaltisme qui puisse conduire à la diarhée ce qui constitue le tableau de quelqu'un

qui a peur. Neamoins on peut aussi faire le tableau d'apercu sur un terrain des maladies cardiovasculaires et dire que un son d'intensité élevée entraine des effects sur le coeur et les vaisseaux se traduisant par des palpitations, une hyper ou paradoxalement une hypotension avec perte de connaissance, une situation qui poura s'aggraver par la fréquence du bruit." (a shot of a bullet, a tire that bursts, a passing aircarft can cause the production of catecholamines, namely adrenaline and noradrenaline in the adrenal gland, which have effects of palpitation, increase in blood pressure , increase peristalsis which can lead to diarrhea. This constitutes the picture of someone who is afraid. However, we can also provide an overview of cardiovascular diseases and say that high intensity of sound causes effects on the heart and vessels resulting in palpitations, hyper or paradoxically hypotension with loss of consciousness, a situation which could be made worse by the frequency of the noise.) On the author's interview file of April 27, 2020.

3 Benedicte A. Claes, Aircraft Noise Regulation in the European Union: The Hushkit Problem, 65 J. Air L. Com. 329, 2000, p 337.

4 Idem.

5 Benedicte A. Claes, Aircraft Noise Regulation in the European Union: The Hushkit Problem, 65 J. Air L. Com. 329, 2000, p 336.

6 However, McNairn rather refers to the 1966 London Conference as the first interna-tional conference, see Colin H. McNairn, Airport Noise Pollution: The Problem and the Regulatory Response, 50 Can. Bar Rev. 248, 1972, p 259.

7 ICAO, Annex 16 to the Convention on International Civil Aviation, Environmental Protection, Volume I Aircraft Noise, pp xi–xii.

8 Appendix B of the Assembly Resolution A33-7, Development of Standards, Recom-mended Practices and Procedures and/or guidance material relating to the quality of the environment.

9 Appendix C of the Assembly Resolution A33-7, Policies and Programmes. based on a "balanced approach" to aircraft noise management.

10 ICAO, Environmental Report 2010. Aviation and Climate Change.

11. See ICAO Guidance on the Balanced Approach to Aircraft Noise Management, Doc 9829 AN/451, 10/10/10 No 1.

12. Appendix E of the Assembly Resolution A33-7, Local noise-related operating restrictions at airports.

13. Annex 16 Vol 1, p xii.

14. The seventh meeting of the Committee on Aviation Environment Protection (CAEP/7), 2007.

15. See for instance Runmin Ji, Xianghua Huang and Xiachun Zhao, Active jet Noise Control of Turbofan Engine Based on Explicit Model Predictive Control, Applied Sciences, 2022, 4874..

16. See ICAO Guidance on the Balanced Approach to Aircraft Noise Management, Doc 9829 AN/451, 4.1.6.

17. Annex 16, Vol I II-1-1 1/1/15 says that noise certification shall be granted or validated by the State of Registry of an aircraft based on satisfactory evidence that the aircraft complies with requirements that are at least equal to the applicable Standards specified in this Annex.

18. See ICAO Assembly as cited in guideline para 5.1.2.

19. Idem para 5.1.1.

20. Annex 16, 6.3.7..

21. Idem, para 6.3.10..

22. https://www.theguardian.com/business/2019/sep/19/airlines-co2-emissions-rising-up -to-70-faster-than-predicted last consulted on June 29, 2023.

23. Idem.

24. Steven J. Davis, Emissions rebound from the COVID-19 pandemic, https://www.nature .com/articles/s41558-022-01332-6, March 31, 2022.

25. Environmental and Energy Study Institute, Fact Sheet, The Growth in Greenhouse Gas Emissions from Commercial Aviation Part 1 of a Series on Airlines and Climate Change, October 2019.
26. E Terrenoire et al., The Contribution of Carbon Dioxide Emissions from the Aviation Sector to Future Climate Change, 14 Environ. Res. Lett. 084019, 2019.
27. Graver et al., CO2 Emissions from commercial aviation, 2018. International Council on Clean Transportation (ICCT). Working Paper 2019-16 https://theicct.org/sites/default /files/publications/ICCT_CO2-commercl-aviation-2018_20190918.pdf These researchers rate such emissions to 2.4 % in 2018, 2019.
28. Paul Stephen Dempsey, Public International Air Law, Second Edition, p 253.
29. Heather L. Miller, Civil Aircraft Emissions and International Treaty Law, 63 J. Air L. Com. 697, 1998, https://scholar.smu.edu/jalc/vol63/iss4/3, p 701.
30. David S. Lee, Aviation Greenhouse Gas Emissions, in ICAO report 2010, p 42.
31. David S. Lee, Aviation Greenhouse Gas Emissions, in ICAO report 2010, p 45.
32. ICAO Annex 16 to the Convention on International Aviation, Environmental Protection, Vol II, Aircraft Engine Emission, 4th ed, July 2017.
33. See A/CONF. 48/14/Rev.1, Report of the United Nations Conference on Human Environment, Stockholm 5-16 June 1972, p 8.
34. ICAO, Annex 16 to the Convention on Civil Aviation, Environment Protection, Vol II, Aircraft Emission, 4th ed, July 2017, p ix.
35. Annex 16, Vol., 2 Part II para 1.2.
36. Annex 16, Vol., 2 Part II para 3.4.

Chapter 4: Security of Aircraft

1. European Parliament, Air transport: Civil aviation security, www.europarl.europa.eu /factsheets/en, last consulted January 26, 2023..
2. J. Nowak, Protection of Air Transport against Acts of Unlawful Interference, What's Next? Proceedings of 23rd International Scientific Conference. Transport Means 2019, p 2.
3. See Brian A. Jackson and David R. Frelinger, The Problem to Be Solved: Aviation Terrorism Risk Past, Present, and Future, in Brian A. Jackson et al., Efficient Aviation Security, Strengthening the Analytic Foundation for Making Air Transportation Security Decisions, RAND Corporation, 2012, p 13.
4. For further reading, See ICAO Council Resolution A33-3: Increasing the effectiveness of ICAO to face new challenges.
5. This Regulation was replaced by Regulation (EC) No 300/2008 of the European Parliament and of the Council of 11 March 2008 on common rules in the field of civil aviation security and repealed Regulation (EC) No 2320/2002.
6. Giovanni Marchiafava, The Montreal Protocol 2014 and Current International Regulation Issues on Aviation Security, 83(2) Riv. Stud. Polit. Int. 235, 2016, p 237 for further reading on the same, see Jangir Arasly, Terrorism and Civil Aviation Security: Problems and Trends, Partnership for Peace Consortium of Defense Academies and Security Studies Institutes, 4(1) Connections 75–90, 2005.
7 Article 1, 1963 Tokyo Convention.
8 Article 3(1) 1963 Tokyo Convention.
9 Article 4, 1963 Tokyo Convention.
10. Article 6, 1963 Tokyo Convention.
11. Article 7, 1963 Tokyo Convention.
12. Article 11, 1963 Tokyo Convention.
13. Preamble, 1970 Hague Convention.
14. Article 1, 1970 Hague Convention.
15. Article 4, 1970 Hague Convention.

16. Article 8(3) 1970 Hague Convention.
17. Article 1(1) a, b 1971 Montreal Convention.
18. Article 1(1) c, d 1971 Montreal Convention.
19. See National Centre for Biotechnology information, https://pubchem.ncbi.nlm.nih.gov last consulted on June 29, 2023.
20. Article 4, 1991 Montreal Convention.
21. Annex 17, 1-1, 1/7/11.
22. Annex 17, 3-1, 1/7/11.
23. Annex 17, 3-3, 1/7/11.
24. Annex 17, 4-1, 1/7/11.
25. Annex 17, 5-1, 1/7/11.
26. Annex 17, 5-2,5.
27. Annex 11, 2.22.1.
28. idem.

Chapter 5: Air Traffic Control Service (ATCS)

1. http://www.atcguild.com/tour/atctour02.asp See Chrystel Erotokritou, The Legal Liability of Air Traffic Controllers, 4 Inquiries J. 1, 2012, last consulted on June 29, 2023.
2. Annex 11, 1/11/01, 1-2.
3. Annex 11, 1/11/01, 2-2.
4. Michael R. Jackson, Yiyuan J. Zhao and Rhonda A. Slattery. Sensitivity of Trajectory Prediction in Air Traffic Management. 22(2) J. Guid. Control Dyn. 219–228, 1999, as cited by S. Hao et al., A Multi-Aircraft Conflict Detection and Resolution Method for 4-dimensional Trajectory-Based Operation, 31(7) Chin. J. Aeronaut. 1579–1593, 2018, p 1580.
5. Annex 11, 3.3.1.
6. Hojjat Emami and Farnaz Derakhshan, A New Method for Conflict Detection and Resolution in Air Traffic Management, AAAI Technical Report WS-12-13, 2012, p 37.
7. Annex 11, 3.3.4.
8. S. Hao et al., A Multi-Aircraft Conflict Detection and Resolution Method for 4-Dimensional Trajectory-Based Operation, 31(7) Chin. J. Aeronaut. 1579–1593, 2018, p 1580.
9. Annex 11 2-1 1/11/01.
10. Annex 11, 2.20.1.
11. Annex 11, 3.5.2.
12. Annex 11, 3.7.1.1.
13. Aviation dictionary. 2014, http://aviation_dictionary.enacademic.com/6473/strayed_aircraft last consulted on June 29, 2023.
14. Idem.
15. Annex 11, 2.23.1.1.
16. CAA Standards & Procedures (ATCIs) Manual - Section 9 Page 10 of 18, 2.1. February 8, 2013.
17. Annex 11, 2.23.1.1.1.
18. Annex 11, 2.23.1.2.

Chapter 6: Aircraft Search and Rescue

1. Annex 12, 1-1.
2. Idem.
3. Annex 12, 1-1.
4. Australian National Search and Rescue Council, National Search and Rescue Manual, September 2018 edition, 2.6.4.

5. Ruwantissa Abeyratne, Search and Rescue Operation of Aircraft in Africa: Some Compelling Issues, 7(3) J. Air Transp. 55–72, 2002, p 58.
6. National Search and Rescue Manual, B–GA–209–001/FP–001, DFO 5449, para 5.18.
7. Australian National Search and Rescue Council, National Search and Rescue Manual, September 2018 edition, 3.2.10.
8. Australian National Search and Rescue Council, National Search and Rescue Manual, September 2018 edition, 3.5.9-10.
9. Boldmethod, The 4 Types of Airspeed, and What Each One Means for You, https://www.boldmethod.com/blog/lists/2019/11/the-four-types-of-airspeed-and-how-each-works/ last consulted on June 29, 2023.
10. Idem.
11. National Search and Rescue Manual 5.69-71.
12. Canadian National Search and Rescue Manual 5.89.
13. Canadian National Search and Rescue Manual 5.91.

Chapter 7: The Rules of the Air

1. Article 12, 1944 Chicago Convention.
2. Annex 2, 2.1.1.
3. Annex 2, 2, 2.
4. https://www.who.int/health-topics/drugs-psychoactive#tab=tab_1 last consulted on June 29, 2023.
5. See Annex 2, Commentary 1.15.
6. See The International Drug Conventions, Tables of the United Nations Convention against Illicit Traffic in Narcotic Drugs and Psychotropic Substance of 1988, as at 23 November 2022.
7. Annex 2, 2.5.
8. Annex 2, 3.2.2.1.
9. Annex 2, 3.2.2.3.
10. Annex 2, 3.2.2.2.
11. Annex 2, 3.2.2.4.
12. Annex 2, 3.2.2.5.2.
13. Article 3 of the UNCLOS provides that "every State has the right to establish the breadth of its territorial sea up to a limit not exceeding 12 nautical miles, measured from baselines determined in accordance with this Convention".
14. Article 57 of the UNCLOS stipulates that "the exclusive economic zone shall not extend beyond 200 nautical miles from the baselines from which the breadth of the territorial sea is measured".
15. Article 77(1) UNCLOS.
16. Jean Carroz, International Legislation on Air Navigation over the High Seas, 26(2) J. Air L. Com. 158, 1959.
17. ICAO Doc 7278-C/841, Definition of Scheduled International Air Service (1952).

Chapter 8: The Warsaw System of Liability

1. It is this body of instruments that could be referred to as the Warsaw System.
2. Article 4 of the 1929 Warsaw Convention.
3. Article 11(2) of the 1929 Warsaw Convention stipulates that "any statements in the air waybill or the cargo receipt relating to the weight, dimensions, and packing of the cargo, as well as those relating to the number of packages, are prima facie evidence of the facts stated; those relating to the quantity, volume, and condition of the cargo do not constitute evidence against the carrier except so far as they both have been, and are

stated in the air waybill or the cargo receipt to have been, checked by it in the presence of the consignor, or relate to the apparent condition of the cargo".

4. According to Article 17(1) of the 1929 Warsaw Convention, the carrier is liable for damage sustained in case of death or bodily injury of a passenger upon condition only that the accident that caused the death or injury took place on board the aircraft or in the course of any of the operations of embarking or disembarking..

5. J. Brent Alldredge, Continuing Questions in Aviation Liability Law: Should Article 17 of the Warsaw Convention Be Construed to Encompass Physical Manifestations of Emotional and Mental Distress, 67 J. Air L. Com 1345, 2002, p 1355.

6. For further comment, see Christopher Andrews et al., Psychiatric Injury in Aviation Accidents under the Warsaw and Montreal Conventions: The Interface between Medicine and Law, 75 J. Air L. Com. 3, 2011 and John F. Easton et al., Post Traumatic Lesion Corporelle: A Continuum of Bodily Injury Under the Warsaw Convention, 68 J. Air L. Com. 665, 2003.

7. Article 17(2) of the 1929 Warsaw Convention.

8. Article 17(3) of the 1929 Warsaw Convention.

9. Article 18(1) of the 1929 Warsaw Convention.

10. Article 18 (2) of the 1929 Warsaw Convention.

11. Article 20 of the 1929 Warsaw Convention.

12. Idem.

13. J. C. Batra, Modernization of the Warsaw System—Montreal 1999, 65 J. Air L. Com. 429, 2000, p 430.

14. 1995 Intercarrier Agreement on Passenger Liability para 1.

15. James N. Fincher, Watching Liability Limits under the Warsaw Convention Fly Away, and the IATA Initiative, 10 Transnat'l Law. 309, 1997, p 321.

16. 1995 Intercarrier Agreement on Passenger Liability para 2.

17. Pablo Mendes De Leon et al., The Montreal Convention: Analysis of Some Aspects of the Attempted Modernization and Consolidation of the Warsaw System, 66 J. Air L. Com. 1155, 2001, p 1172.

18. An illustration of the application of this regulation can be found in the Lufthansa General Terms & Conditions – Conditions of Carriage for Passengers and Baggage (flight ticket GCC) According to which. There are no maximum compensation amounts for liability in the event of the death or injury of passengers. For damages of up to SDR 128.821 the airline company shall not be able to contest claims for damages concerning fault. It further states that the air carrier can defend itself against claims that exceed the above amount if it can prove that it neither acted negligently nor was otherwise at fault.

19. Lisa Tomas, Air Transport Agreements, Regulation of Liability, Max-Planck Encyclopedia of International Law.

20. J. C. Batra, Modernization of the Warsaw System—Montreal 1999, 65 J. Air L. Com. 429, 2000, p 438.

21. See Article 19 1999 Montreal Convention.

22. See Article 22 (1) 1999 Montreal Convention.

23. See Article 22 (2) 1999 Montreal Convention.

24. See Article 22 (3) 1999 Montreal Convention.

Chapter 9: The International Civil Aviation Organization (ICAO)

1. See The International Civil Aviation Conference, Final Act and Related Documents, Washington 1945.

2. Section 3 of the Interim Agreement on International Civil Aviation.

3. PMJ Mendes de Leon, International Civil Aviation Organization (ICAO), Max-Planck Encyclopedia of International Law, para 5.

4. https://www.icao.int/secretariat/RegionalOffice/Pages/default.aspx last consulted on June 29, 2023.
5. See UNGA Res 50(I) of 14 December 1946 on agreement with special agencies.
6. This is equally stipulated in Rule 1 of the Standing Rules of the Assembly of ICAO, which states, "The Assembly shall meet not less than once in three years and shall be convened by the Council at a suitable time and place".
7. See Rule 2 of the Standing Rules of the Assembly of ICAO, which states, "The Assembly may hold extraordinary sessions at any time upon the call of the Council or at the request of not less than one-fifth of the total number of Contracting States addressed to the Secretary-General".
8. See Rule 43 of the Standing Rules of the Assembly of ICAO.
9. See Rule 28 of the Standing Rules of the Assembly of ICAO.
10. See Administrative package for ratification of the Protocol amending Article 50(A) of the Convention on International Civil Aviation (2016).
11. ICAO, Aviation Navigation Commission Special 200th Session Commemorative Review, 2015, p 3.
12. See Article 56 of the 1944 Chicago Convention.
13. PMJ Mendes de Leon, International Civil Aviation Organization (ICAO), Max-Planck Encyclopedia of International Law, para 33.
14. See article 38, 1944 Chicago Convention.
15. See article 90(a), 1944 Chicago Convention.
16. The same has been captured by Rule 1 of the Rules for the settlements of differences approved by the Council on 9 April 1957 and amended on 10 November 1975, according to which, "(1)The Rules of Parts I and III shall govern the settlement of the following disagreements between Contracting States, which may be referred to the Council:
(a) Any disagreement between two or more Contracting States relating to the interpretation or application of the Convention on International Civil Aviation (hereinafter called ·the Convention') and its Annexes (Articles 84 to 88 of the Convention).
(b) Any disagreement between two or more Contracting States relating to the interpretation or application of the International Air Services Transit Agreement and of the International Air Transport Agreement (hereinafter respectively called ·Transit Agreement' and ·Transport Agreement') (Article 11, Section 2 of the Transit Agreement; Article IV, Section 3 of the Transport Agreement).
(2) The Rules of Parts I and III shall govern the consideration of any complaint regarding an action taken by a State party to the Transit Agreement and under that Agreement, which another State party to the same Agreement deems to cause injustice or hardship to it (Article 11, Section I), or regarding a similar action under the Transport Agreement (Article IV, Section 2).".
17. The cases are India v. Pakistan (1952), Great Britain v. Spain (1967), Pakistan v. India (1971), Cuba v. USA (1998), USA v. EU (2000), Brazil v. USA (2016), Qatar v. Bahrain, Egypt, UAE, and Saudi Arabia (2017).
18. Dmitry V. Ivanov and Vladislav G. Donakanian, The ICAO Council as a Dispute Settlement Body: Theoretical and Practical Issues, (3) Moscow J. Int. Law 33, 2022.
19. Section 1 of the Air Services Agreement dated 23 June 1948 provides that: "Each contracting State grants to the other contracting States the following freedoms of the air in respect of scheduled international air services:
(1) The privilege to fly across its territory without landing;
(2) The privilege to land for non-traffic purposes."
20. See International Court of Justice Appeal relating to the jurisdiction of the ICAO Council, India v. Pakistan, Pleadings oral arguments documents 18.
21. See International Court of Justice Appeal relating to the jurisdiction of the ICAO Council, India v. Pakistan, counter-memorial submitted by the Government of Pakistan, para 21.

22. See International Court of Justice Appeal relating to the jurisdiction of the ICAO Council, India v. Pakistan, Judgment of 18 August 1972 para 36.
23. See International Court of Justice Appeal relation to the jurisdiction of the ICAO Council under Article 84 of the Convention on International Civil Aviation (Bahrain, Egypt, Saudi Arabia, and United Arab Emirates v. Qatar) Judgment of July 14, 2020, para 21.

Chapter 10: The International Air Transport Association

1. See Act of Incorporation, An Act to Incorporate the International Air Transport Association, Statutes of Canada, 1945, Chapter 51 (Assented to December 18, 1945) as amended from time to time.
2. See article 4 of the Articles.
3. See article 2 of the Articles.
4. Peter PC Haanappel, International Air Transport Association (IATA), Max-Planck Encyclopedia of International Law, para 9.
5. For further details see McGraw-Hill, Dictionary of Scientific & Technical Terms, 6th ed, The McGraw-Hill Companies, Inc. 2003.
6. See Rule 1 of the Rules of Procedure of the General Meeting.
7. See Rule 2.
8. Article 5(6)(b)(i) of the Articles.
9. See article 14(1) of the Articles.
10. See Rule II of the Rules and Regulations.
11. Idem.
12. Rules and Regulations of the Advisory Councils As of 19 June 2022.
13. For further details, see Lasantha Hettiarachchi, The Quasi-Regulatory Regime of the International Air Transport Association (IATA) and Its Impact upon the Airline Industry and the Consumer, Institute of Air and Space Law, McGill University, 2018.
14. Peter PC Haanappel, International Air Transport Association (IATA), Max-Planck Encyclopedia of International Law, para 17.

BIBLIOGRAPHY

Published Books and Articles

Ruwantissa Abeyratne, Search and Rescue Operation of Aircraft in Africa: Some Compelling Issues, 7(3) J. Air Transp. 55–72, 2002

Christopher Andrews et al., Psychiatric Injury in Aviation Accidents under the Warsaw and Montreal Conventions: The Interface between Medicine and Law, 75 J. Air L. Com. 3, 2011

J. C. Batra, Modernization of the Warsaw System—Montreal 1999, 65 J. Air L. Com. 429, 2000

J. Brent Alldredge, Continuing Questions in Aviation Liability Law: Should Article 17 of the Warsaw Convention Be Construed to Encompass Physical Manifestations of Emotional and Mental Distress, 67 J. Air L. Com. 1345, 2002

Jean Carroz, International Legislation on Air Navigation over the High Seas, 26(2) J. Air L. Com. 158, 1959

Bin Cheng, Studies in International Air Law, Brill Nijhoff, 2018

Benedicte A. Claes, Aircraft Noise Regulation in the European Union: The Hushkit Problem, 65 J. Air L. Com. 329, 2000

John Cobb Cooper, The International Air Navigation Conference, 19(2) J. Air L. Com. 127, 1952

Pablo Mendes De Leon et al., The Montreal Convention: Analysis of Some Aspects of the Attempted Modernization and Consolidation of the Warsaw System, 66 J. Air L. Com. 1155, 2001

PMJ Mendes de Leon, International Civil Aviation Organization (ICAO), Max-Planck Encyclopedia of International Law, 2007

Paul Stephen Dempsey, Public International Air Law, 2nd ed, 2017

Marc L. J. Dierikx, Shaping World Aviation: Anglo-American Civil Aviation Relations, 1944-1946, 57 J. Air L. Com. 795, 1992

John F. Easton et al., Post Traumatic Lesion Corporelle: A Continuum of Bodily Injury Under the Warsaw Convention, 68 J. Air L. Com. 665, 2003

Hojjat Emami and Farnaz Derakhshan, A New Method for Conflict Detection and Resolution in Air Traffic Management, AAAI Technical Report WS-12-13, 2012

Environmental and Energy Study Institute, Fact Sheet, The Growth in Greenhouse Gas Emissions from Commercial Aviation Part 1 of a Series on Airlines and Climate Change, October 2019

Chrystel Erotokritou, The Legal Liability of Air Traffic Controllers, 4 Inquiries J. 1, 2012

James N. Fincher, Watching Liability Limits under the Warsaw Convention Fly Away, and the IATA Initiative, 10 Transnat'l Law. 309, 1997

Elmar M. Giemulla, Cabotage, Max-Planck Encyclopedia of International Law, 2012

Peter PC Haanappel, International Air Transport Association (IATA), Max-Planck Encyclopedia of International Law, 2009

P. P. Haanappel, Bilateral Air Transport Agreements—1913-1980, 5 Md. J. Int'l L. 241, 1980

Lasantha Hettiarachchi, The Quasi-Regulatory Regime of the International Air Transport Association (IATA) and Its Impact upon the Airlines Industry and the Consumer, Institute of Air and Space Law, McGill University, 2018

ICAO Guidance on the Balanced Approach to Aircraft Noise Management, Doc 9829 AN/451

ICAO, Aviation Navigation Commission Special 200th Session Commemorative Review, 2015

ICAO, Environmental Report 2010. Aviation and Climate Change

Dmitry V. Ivanov and Vladislav G. Donakanian, The ICAO Council as a Dispute Settlement Body: Theoretical and Practical Issues, (3) Moscow J. Int. Law 33, 2022

Brian A. Jackson and David R. Frelinger, The Problem to Be Solved: Aviation Terrorism Risk Past, Present, and Future, in Brian A. Jackson et al., Efficient Aviation Security, Strengthening the Analytic Foundation for Making Air Transportation Security Decisions, RAND Corporation, 2012

Michael R. Jackson, Yiyuan J. Zhao, and Rhonda A. Slattery. Sensitivity of Trajectory Prediction in Air Traffic Management, 22(2) J. Guid. Control Dyn. 219–228, 1999

Alan Khee-Jin Tan, Singapore's New Air Services Agreements with the E.U. and the U.K.: Implications for Liberalization in Asia, 73 J. Air L. Com. 351, 2008

Stephen Latchford, Habana Convention on Commercial Aviation, 2 J. Air L. Com. 207–210, 1931

David S. Lee, Aviation Greenhouse Gas Emissions, in ICAO report 2010

Antigoni Lykotrafiti, Consolidation and Rationalization in the Transatlantic Air Transport Market—Prospects and Challenges for Competition and Consumer Welfare, 76 J. Air L. Com. 661, 2011

Giovanni Marchiafava, The Montreal Protocol 2014 and Current International Regulation Issues on Aviation Security, 83(2) Riv. Stud. Polit. Int. 235, 2016

L. Q. Maurice, D. S. Lee (eds), Assessing Current Scientific Knowledge, Uncertainties and Gaps in Quantifying Climate Change, Noise and Air Quality Aviation Impacts, 2009

McGraw-Hill, Dictionary of Scientific & Technical Terms, 6th ed, The McGraw Hill Companies, Inc. 2003

Arnold D. McNair, The Beginnings and the Growth of Aeronautical Law, 1 J. Air L. Com. 383, 1930

Colin H. McNairn, Airport Noise Pollution: The Problem and the Regulatory Response, 50 Can. Bar Rev. 248, 1972

Michael Milde, International Air Law and ICAO, Eleven International Publishing, 2017

Heather L. Miller, Civil Aircraft Emissions and International Treaty Law, 63 J. Air L. Com. 697, 1998

J. Nowak, Protection of Air Transport against Acts of Unlawful Interference, What's Next? Proceedings of 23rd International Scientific Conference. Transport Means 2019

Louis Rolland, L'accord Franco-Allemand du 26 juillet 1913 relatif à la navigation aérienne, A. Pedone, 1913

Albert Roper, Recent Developments in International Aeronautical Law, 1 J. Air L. Com. 395, 1930

Lisa Tomas, Air Transport Agreements, Regulation of Liability, Max-Planck Encyclopedia of International Law

Diederiks-Verschoor, Introduction to Air Law, Wolters Kluwer, 2012

Alfred Wegerdt, Germany and the Aerial Navigation Convention at Paris, October 13, 1919, 1 J. Air L. Com. 1, 1930

Jan Wouters, Sten Verhoeven, State Aircraft, Max-Planck Encyclopedia of International Public Law

Legal and Quasi-Legal Sources

Regulation (EC) No 300/2008 of the European Parliament and of the Council of 11 March 2008 on common rules in the field of civil aviation security and repealing Regulation (EC) No 2320/2002

Rules and Regulations of the Advisory Councils as of 19 June 2022

1929 Convention for the Unification of Certain Rules Relating to International Carriage by Air

1933 Rome Convention on Aircraft Operator Liability for Surface Damage

1944 Chicago Convention on Safety Navigation

1948 Geneva Convention on Aircraft Registration

1952 Rome Convention Aircraft Operator Liability for Surface Damage

1955 Protocol to Amend the Convention for the Unification of Certain Rules Relating to International Carriage by Air Signed at Warsaw on 12 October 1929

1961 Convention, Supplementary to the Warsaw Convention, for the Unification of Certain Rules Relating to International Carriage by Air Performed by a Person Other than the Contracting Carrier

1963 Tokyo Convention on Offenses on Board Aircraft

1970 Hague Convention Aircraft Hijack

1971 Additional Protocol Nos. 1 to 3 and Montreal Protocol No. 4 to amend the Warsaw Convention as amended by The Hague Protocol or the Warsaw Convention as amended by both The Hague Protocol and the Guatemala City

1971 Montreal Convention on Aircraft and Air Navigation Security

1971 Protocol to Amend the Convention for the Unification of Certain Rules Relating to International Carriage by Air Signed at Warsaw on 12 October 1929 as Amended by the Protocol Done at The Hague on 28 September 1955 Signed at Guatemala City on 8 March 1971

1975 Montreal Protocols Amending the Warsaw Convention

1999 Montreal Convention on Carrier Liability to Passengers and in Respect of Cargo

1999 The Convention for the Unification of Certain Rules for International Carriage by Air

2001 Cape Town Convention on Financial Interest in Aircraft

2009 Montreal Conventions on Aircraft Operator Liability for Surface Damage

2010 Beijing Convention and Its Protocol on Aviation Security

2014 Montreal Protocol Amending the Tokyo Convention of 1963

Act of Incorporation, An Act to Incorporate the International Air Transport Association, Statutes of Canada, 1945

www.ingramcontent.com/pod-product-compliance
Lightning Source LLC
Chambersburg PA
CBHW020331220326
41518CB00046B/671